PATHFINDER
PLAYER COMPANION

Development Lead · James Jacobs
Authors · Alexander Augunas, Russ Brown, John Compton, Alex Riggs, David Ross
Cover Artist · Miroslav Petrov
Interior Artists · Graey Erb, Veli Nyström, and Bryan Syme

Editor-in-Chief · F. Wesley Schneider
Creative Director · James Jacobs
Creative Design Director · Sarah E. Robinson
Executive Editor · James L. Sutter
Senior Developer · Rob McCreary
Pathfinder Society Lead Developer · John Compton
Developers · Adam Daigle, Crystal Frasier, Amanda Hamon Kunz, Mark Moreland, Owen K.C. Stephens, and Linda Zayas-Palmer
Managing Editor · Judy Bauer
Senior Editor · Christopher Carey
Editors · Jason Keeley, Elisa Mader, and Josh Vogt
Lead Designer · Jason Bulmahn
Designers · Logan Bonner, Stephen Radney-MacFarland, and Mark Seifter
Art Director · Sonja Morris
Senior Graphic Designers · Emily Crowell and Adam Vick

Publisher · Erik Mona
Paizo CEO · Lisa Stevens
Chief Operations Officer · Jeffrey Alvarez
Director of Sales · Pierce Watters
Sales Associate · Cosmo Eisele
Marketing Director · Jenny Bendel
Chief Financial Officer · John Parrish
Staff Accountant · Ashley Kaprielian
Data Entry Clerk · B. Scott Keim
Chief Technical Officer · Vic Wertz
Software Development Manager · Cort Odekirk
Senior Software Developer · Gary Teter
Project Manager · Jessica Price
Organized Play Coordinator · Tonya Woldridge
Adventure Card Game Designer · Tanis O'Connor

Community Team · Liz Courts and Chris Lambertz
Customer Service Team · Sharaya Copas, Katina Davis, Sara Marie Teter, and Diego Valdez
Warehouse Team · Laura Wilkes Carey, Will Chase, Mika Hawkins, Heather Payne, Jeff Strand, and Kevin Underwood
Website Team · Christopher Anthony, William Ellis, Lissa Guillet, Don Hayes, Julie Iaccarino, and Erik Keith

ON THE COVER

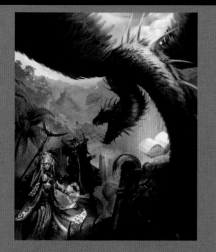

While exploring the ruins of a temple deep in the jungle, Alahazra and Imrijka encounter a divine couatl in this tense cover by Miroslav Petrov.

TABLE OF CONTENTS

REFERENCE

This book refers to several other Pathfinder Roleplaying Game products using the following abbreviations, yet these additional supplements are not required to make use of this book. Readers interested in references to Pathfinder RPG hardcovers can find the complete rules of these books available online for free at **paizo.com/prd**.

Advanced Class Guide	ACG	*Ultimate Combat*	UC
Advanced Player's Guide	APG	*Ultimate Intrigue*	UI
Inner Sea Gods	ISG	*Ultimate Magic*	UM
Occult Adventures	OA		

paizo

Paizo Inc.
7120 185th Ave NE, Ste 120
Redmond, WA 98052-0577

paizo.com

This product is compliant with the Open Game License (OGL) and is suitable for use with the Pathfinder Roleplaying Game or the 3.5 edition of the world's oldest fantasy roleplaying game.

Product Identity: The following items are hereby identified as Product Identity, as defined in the Open Game License version 1.0a, Section 1(e), and are not Open Content: All trademarks, registered trademarks, proper names (characters, deities, etc.), dialogue, plots, storylines, locations, characters, artwork, and trade dress. (Elements that have previously been designated as Open Game Content or are in the public domain are not included in this declaration.)

Open Content: Except for material designated as Product Identity (see above), the game mechanics of this Paizo game product are Open Game Content, as defined in the Open Gaming License version 1.0a Section 1(d). No portion of this work other than the material designated as Open Game Content may be reproduced in any form without written permission.

Introduction

Throughout Golarion's history, legends tell of faithful agents of the divine who directly communed with their patron deities. Blessed with purpose and direction, these individuals are among the most influential members of their faith ever to live. Most of the faithful, however, never meet their deity face-to-face, and as a result, they rely on the lessons and aphorisms of their traditions and words recorded within religious tomes. Rather than enshrining the interpretation of a single cleric or prophet, most prayer books combine the collected wisdom of centuries of deific worship and tradition, offering a continuity of belief that exceeds that of any individual soul.

Using Prayer Books

In the Inner Sea region, tomes dedicated to widely accepted rites and practices of a given faith are known as holy texts. Although exact sizes vary, most holy texts weigh 2 pounds and cost 25 gp. A subcategory of these tomes are known as prayer books—these are generally higher-quality holy texts that can come in virtually any size (although most are similar in size to typical holy texts). Prayer books can be embellished with precious metals and stones, use stronger paper that is resistant to damage, or contain particularly poetic and lyrical prose. Any such enhancements can elevate a prayer book to the status of a work of art, with no upper end to the price such a treasure might command. Other prayer books are so well organized and concise that

the use of such a tome in conjunction with research grants a +2 circumstance bonus on a Knowledge (religion) check, akin to the way other masterwork tools enhance other skill checks. A prayer book that grants such a boon costs an additional 100 gp above its base cost.

The primary purpose of a prayer book is to contain details on rare or unusual divine spells, obscure feats, fighting styles, formulae for the crafting of magic items, information about esoteric methods of worship, and more. *Pathfinder Player Companion: Divine Anthology* explores several different examples of these rare and valuable prayer books, along with the specialized character options they contain. *Pathfinder Player Companion: Arcane Anthology* contains additional information about prayer books.

Deity-Specific Holy Texts

Most deities have at least one holy text or prayer book directly associated with their worship—*Pathfinder Campaign Setting: Inner Sea Gods* lists details on the core 20 deities' most famous holy texts. At the GM's discretion, some copies of these holy texts may function as prayer books, contain additional spells or character options, and offer worshipers of specific deities ways to gain appropriate character options presented in this book, as seems appropriate for the content.

The Acts of Iomedae (Iomedae): This tome describes the Inheritor's greatest acts of service to Aroden.

Asmodean Monograph (Asmodeus): This massive tome covers religious rites, lessons on writing contracts, and musings on the nature of power.

The Birth of Light and Truth (Sarenrae): This tome contains stories dating before Sarenrae's ascension.

The Book of Joy (Calistria): This tome describes methods to manipulate others.

The Book of Magic (Nethys): This tome serves as a comprehensive spellcasting guide.

The Bones Land in a Spiral (Pharasma): This holy text was written by an ancient prophet, and no one is certain what it foretells.

Cycle of the Beast (Rovagug): This text was penned by a mad prophet in his own blood.

The Eight Scrolls (Desna): These eight doctrines summarize Desna's deific mythos, tenets, and philosophy.

The Four Hides of Lawm (Lamashtu): This profane scripture describes the teachings of Lamashtu.

Gorumskagat (Gorum): This epic poem describes the creed of Gorum's church.

Hammer and Tongs: The Forging of Metal and Other Good Works (Torag): Torag's holy text includes the history of the dwarven race.

Hymns to the Wind and the Waves (Gozreh): This collection of prayers guides Gozreh's flock in showing reverence for nature.

Melodies of Inner Beauty (Shelyn): The tome details stories about Shelyn through hymns and poetry.

The Order of Numbers (Abadar): This regimented tome includes hundreds of laws and customs.

Parables of Erastil (Erastil): Locals often adapt this practical tome to suit their way of life.

Placard of Wisdom (Cayden Cailean): This simple placard teaches Cayden's lessons using colloquialisms.

Serving Your Hunger (Urgathoa): Urgathoa's prayer book lauds the greatness of self-serving sensation.

Umbral Leaves (Zon-Kuthon): Zon-Kuthon's prayer book is a tome of his tenets and laws, and is often made from flayed skin.

Unbinding the Fetters (Irori): This lengthy tome contains a variety of training regimens.

The Words Behind the Mask (Norgorber): This coded book comprises 17 smaller tomes.

WARPRIESTS AND VARIANT SPELLCASTING

Pathfinder Campaign Setting: Inner Sea Gods presents rules for variant spellcasting that grant clerics of the 20 core deities access to a few spells that normally aren't available to clerics (for example, clerics of Sarenrae can prepare *sunbeam* as a 7th-level spell), or early access to more powerful spells (for example, clerics of Zon-Kuthon can prepare *symbol of pain* as a 4th-level spell). Warpriests, as a hybrid class of cleric and fighter, should be treated as clerics in this regard for determining what variant spellcasting options are available to them depending on the deity they worship.

RULES INDEX

Pathfinder Player Companion: Divine Anthology introduces a wide range of new rules content that covers numerous options for your character. Of course, many of these elements are excellent choices for clerics or other divine spellcasters, but this book assumes that other types of characters may also be devoted followers of the gods or religious philosophies. As a result, many options found within this book are intended for arcane or psychic spellcasters and non-spellcasters. All of this exciting content awaits in the following pages—have fun exploring and finding something new for your character!

The Majestic Book of the Prime Ascended

The list of women and men who have transcended their own mortality and ascended to godhood is a short one indeed, but *The Majestic Book of the Prime Ascended* exalts five such individuals of this august assembly above the others as exemplars of certain virtues to which humanity should aspire. The ascended gods Cayden Cailean, Iomedae, Irori, Nethys, and Norgorber are all cited as paragons for the faithful to emulate and perhaps to follow into divinity.

The book was written by Theodrenne Armande, a Taldan religious scholar living in the Ascendant Court of Absalom in 4214 AR. Armande was virtually unknown at the time, even in theological circles, and *The Majestic Book of the Prime Ascended* was the single major work she produced in her lifetime. This has led some scholars to speculate that she may have been a surrogate for the book's true author, who wished to remain anonymous. *The Majestic Book of the Prime Ascended* is most well known in Absalom itself, especially among candidates preparing for the Test of the *Starstone* and their followers. Abridged copies of the prayer book (lacking most of the class option information) can be found in many stalls along the Avenue of the Hopeful. The book can also be found in most of the larger cities in the Inner Sea region and is particularly well known in regions where worship of one of the prime ascended is already widespread.

The views espoused in *The Majestic Book of the Prime Ascended* are far from universally accepted. Indeed, to some, the words contained within are offensive or even blasphemous. Priests of Milani, for example, find the book's claims to be preposterous, as they believe it slights the Everbloom by omitting her from consideration. The book is utterly banned in the nation of Razmiran for its failure to include Razmir as one of the prime ascended. Of course, all holy texts and prayer books are banned within the borders of Rahadoum, but the Council of Elders takes an especially dim view of *The Majestic Book of the Prime Ascended* since it encourages the belief that mortals should aspire to divinity.

The book is organized into five separate chapters, each one focusing on a different deity. Theodrenne Armande concentrates on a single thematic aspect of each ascended god or goddess to hold up as an example to which mortals should aspire. While the volume was intended to be one self-contained work, in subsequent printings some individual chapters have been published as separate volumes. This usually occurs when demand for a single section outweighs the demand for others in certain areas.

With the exception of the chapter on Irori, each section in *The Majestic Book of the Prime Ascended* contains advice on the creation of a specific magical item. Owning this book (or the appropriate chapter) allows a crafter to ignore all of the spell requirements for crafting the item in question.

Prime Archmage, The All-Seeing-Eye

Legends from ancient Osirion tell of the god-king Nethys and his relentless quest for ever-increasing magical knowledge and innovation. That quest culminated in his gaze piercing the secrets of reality, an event that resulted in his ascent to divinity. *The Majestic Book of the Prime Ascended* praises Nethys for his persistence and devotion in this search for magical knowledge. This chapter in the holy text encourages his mortal followers to emulate those qualities in their own lives, especially promoting the pursuit of intellectual or arcane research. Several essays emphasize the importance of developing the theoretical knowledge discovered through research into practical uses in the form of new spells and rituals.

The "Prime Archmage" chapter is particularly well regarded in areas of widespread worship of Nethys and usage of magic, especially Nex and Osirion. Alchemists, arcanists, scholars, and wizards alike seek out this chapter for its philosophical and theological views, as well as its many practical insights into arcane study and research.

Prime Archmage Magic Item

A detailed appendix to "Prime Archmage" outlines the construction requirements for a powerful magical staff.

STAFF OF NETHYS		PRICE 131,550 GP
SLOT none	**CL** 13th	**WEIGHT** 5 lbs.
AURA strong abjuration		

These staves are often made of darkwood and topped with the holy symbol of Nethys, the eyes of which are made of rare gems that glow with magical energy. While the upper end of the staff (along with its symbol) always appears clean and pristine, the lower end of the staff's shaft appears charred by fire and pitted by acid. This staff allows the use of the following spells:

- *Arcane sight* (1 charge)
- *Channel the gift*[ISG] (1 charge)
- *Fractions of heal and harm*[ISG] (1 charge)
- *Spell gauge*[ISG] (1 charge)
- *Prying eyes* (2 charges)
- *Spell scourge*[ISG] (3 charges)

In addition, the wielder of the staff can store additional spells in the staff itself, similarly to a ring of spell storing. The staff of Nethys can contain up to 5 levels of spells (arcane, divine, or psychic, or even a mix of all three). The wielder doesn't need to spend charges to cast one of these stored spells from the staff, but must have levels in a class with that spell on its spell list.

CONSTRUCTION REQUIREMENTS	COST 65,775 GP

Create Staff, Heightened Spell, *arcane sight, channel the gift*ISG or *imbue with spell ability, fractions of heal and harm*ISG, *prying eyes, spell gauge*ISG, *spell scourge*ISG

PRIME ARCHMAGE SPELL

In addition to several sight-based spells, this particularly rare one can be found in "Prime Archmage."

MEDUSA'S BANE

School abjuration; **Level** sorcerer/wizard 4, witch 4
Casting Time 1 standard action
Components V, S, M (tiny fragment
  of a mirror)
Range personal
Target you
Duration 1 round/level

This spell causes your eyes to take on a silvery mirror-like quality, transforming your eyes into metallic-looking orbs that reflect the world you see. Your vision is in no way impaired while this spell is in effect, but you are granted immunity to gaze attacks for the spell's duration. As an immediate action, you can reflect a creature's gaze back on itself, forcing the target of the gaze attack to save against its own gaze weapon or be affected by it. This reflection bypasses the typical immunity creatures with gaze attacks have to their own race's gaze attack, but does not bypass any other resistances or immunities the creature might have. Once you choose to reflect a gaze attack in this manner, the effect of *medusa's bane* immediately ends.

PRIME ARCHMAGE SPELLBOOK

"Prime Archmage" contains several arcane spells, and the chapter itself can function as a spellbook, complete with a preparation ritual (*Pathfinder RPG Ultimate Magic* 121). The methods of magic within these pages focus on spells and effects that enhance vision or otherwise interact with sight, using Nethys' reputation as the All-Seeing Eye as a thematic core. When this section is copied into a separate spellbook, it is often referred to as *The Prying Eye*.

THE PRYING EYE (SPELLBOOK, LEVEL 7 UNIVERSALIST)

The front cover of this tome is as black as night, while the back cover is ivory white. An eye-shaped symbol graces both covers.
Opposition Schools enchantment, necromancy
Value 1,940 gp (2,200 gp with preparation ritual)

SPELLS
4th—*arcane eye, eyes of the void*ACG, *medusa's bane*
3rd—*arcane sight, channel the gift*ISG, *fractions of heal and harm*ISG
2nd—*darkvision, burning gaze*APG, *see invisibility, spell gauge*ISG
1st—*countless eyes*UM, *detect secret doors, identify, invisibility alarm*ACG, *see alignment*UC, *true strike*

PREPARATION RITUAL
Keen Perception (Su) You can spend this boon to gain a +2 insight bonus on a single Perception or Sense Motive check.

PRIME COMMANDER, THE INHERITOR

After completing her legendary tasks while in the service of Aroden, Iomedae passed the Test of the *Starstone* and ascended to divinity. In the last century since Aroden's death, Iomedae has come more fully into her role as a goddess. *The Majestic Book of the Prime Ascended* praises

Iomedae primarily as a leader in her aspect as the goddess of rule and justice, and emphasizes the Inheritor's role as a force for civilization and order rather than focusing on her as a crusader against evil. However, since the two portrayals aren't necessarily at odds with each other, this chapter hasn't yet led to any theological arguments within the Church of Iomedae in the way that "Prime Conspirator" has with the church of Norgorber. Iomedae's chapter, "Prime Commander," resonates strongly with the Mendevian crusaders fighting against the demonic forces of the Worldwound, but the chapter also found popularity in Sargava where Iomedae's worship is on the rise.

Iomedaean Enforcer (Paladin Archetype)

Since the publication of *The Majestic Book of the Prime Ascended*, certain paladins have taken "Prime Commander" to heart and have developed their own methods of upholding the teachings in this book. Iomedaean enforcers have altered abilities that allow them to stand against the forces of chaos. They seek to maintain order and uphold the laws of just rulers and governments, pursuing any who break those laws or otherwise disrupt the peace. Still, they remain lawful good servants of Iomedae, and as such always seek to temper the justice they deliver with mercy.

Class Skills: The Iomedaean enforcer's class skills are Craft (Int), Handle Animal (Cha), Heal (Wis), Intimidate (Cha), Knowledge (local) (Int), Knowledge (religion) (Int), Profession (Wis), Ride (Dex), Sense Motive (Wis), and Spellcraft (Int).

This replaces the paladin's class skills list.

Detect Chaos (Sp): At will, an Iomedaean enforcer can use *detect chaos*, as per the spell. The Iomedaean enforcer can, as a move action, concentrate on a single item or individual within 60 feet and determine whether it is chaotic, learning the strength of its aura as if she had studied it for 3 rounds. While focusing on one individual or object, the Iomedaean enforcer can't use *detect chaos* on any other object or individual within range.

This ability replaces *detect evil*.

Smite Chaos (Su): This ability functions as the paladin's smite evil ability, but against chaotic-aligned creatures. Smite chaos is twice as effective against chaotic-aligned aberrations, outsiders with the chaotic subtype, and fey.

This ability replaces smite evil.

Aura of Order: At 14th level, the paladin's weapons are treated as lawful-aligned for the purposes of overcoming damage reduction. Any attack made against an enemy within 10 feet of the Iomedaean enforcer is treated as if it were lawful-aligned for the purpose of overcoming damage reduction.

This ability alters aura of faith.

Armor of Law (Su): When an enforcer gains damage reduction from aura of righteousness, it is DR 5/chaos instead of DR 5/evil. When that DR increases from the holy champion class feature, it increases to DR 10/chaos.

This ability alters the aura of righteousness and holy champion class features.

Prime Commander Feat

The essays written in "Prime Commander" stress absolute mastery over the field of battle, especially when maintained through teamwork.

Crowd Control (Combat, Teamwork)

You and your allies have been trained to prevent enemies from moving around or through your formation.

Prerequisite: Base attack bonus +3.

Benefit: You gain a +2 competence bonus to your CMD when an enemy uses Acrobatics to move through a square you threaten. For each ally within your reach that also has this feat, the bonus increases by an additional 2.

Prime Commander Magic Item

Those who read "Prime Commander" thoroughly can discover the blueprints for the creation of a powerful magic shield.

ICON OF ORDER		PRICE 26,170 GP
SLOT none	CL 9th	WEIGHT 15 lbs.
AURA moderate abjuration		

An *icon of order* is a *+2 heavy steel shield* that typically displays the sword-and-sunburst holy symbol of Iomedae on a white field. The wielder of an *icon of order* gains a +2 sacred bonus on saves against spells and effects with the chaotic descriptor. Once per day, the wielder can cast *protection from chaos* as a swift action.

CONSTRUCTION REQUIREMENTS	COST 13,170 GP

Craft Magic Arms and Armor, Quicken Spell, *protection from chaos*

Prime Conspirator, Reaper of Reputation

When the ascended god of killers and spies emerged from the Starstone Cathedral, he proceeded to wipe all knowledge of his mortal life from the memories of anyone who possessed it—even the other gods. As a result, little is truly known about Norgorber's history. *The Majestic Book of the Prime Ascended* focuses on this aspect of Norgorber in its second chapter, exploring the mysteries of the god of secrets in his aspect as the Reaper of Reputation. The holy book praises Norgorber for protecting secret knowledge, both his own secrets and the secrets of others by acting as a conspirator. It is unclear whether author Theodrenne Armande was unaware that followers of Norgorber often learn the secrets of others with the express purpose of using that knowledge against them. The text is silent on that subject and seems to express a sincere belief that acting as a conspirator is a worthy pursuit, and many critics have noted that the information presented suggests a fundamental lack of understanding of Norgorber's actual teachings. Unlike the other four chapters, whose associated religions tend to accept the words within as having value and insight to their faiths, worshipers of Norgorber often deride the contents of "Prime Conspirator" as heresies—or apocryphal at best. Regardless, the techniques detailed within the chapter can certainly aid worshipers of Norgorber, or anyone interested in the pursuit of keeping or learning secrets. This chapter is popular in Absalom, but also in Galt where the turbulence of the Red Revolution means uncovering and keeping secrets is a matter of survival.

Prime Conspirator Arcanist Exploit

Information in this chapter of *The Majestic Book of the Prime Ascended* grants arcanists the ability to learn the following arcanist exploit.

Obfuscated Spellcasting (Su): When casting a spell, the arcanist can spend 1 point from her arcane reservoir to make the spell being cast appear to be a different spell. The spell can be disguised as any other spell that the arcanist knows. This exploit raises the DC for a Spellcraft check to correctly identify the spell being cast by double the arcanist's caster level. Identification attempts that fail by an amount less than double the arcanist's caster level mistakenly identify the spell being cast as the false spell chosen by the arcanist.

Prime Conspirator Magic Item

Careful study of information contained in "Prime Conspirator" reveals instructions for creating an item useful to those who collaborate in the shadows.

BOOK OF WRITTEN WHISPERS		PRICE 6,000 GP
SLOT none	CL 3rd	WEIGHT 1 lb.
AURA faint transmutation		

When first created, a *book of written whispers* is a relatively slim volume of blank pages. Typically, the cover of a book of written whispers is made to appear nondescript or plain, but the actual design of the book's cover has no bearing on the item's use. This magic item is used to pen secret messages to allies in distant areas. Each book of whispers is linked to a specific activation word. The backside of each of the book's pages can be removed as a standard action; the removed page appears as a normal piece of paper, and the front side of the page that remains in the book of whispers turns uniformly dark gray. The removed page is known as a "secret letter," while the page from which it was removed is known as a "source page." A secret letter doesn't radiate magic, behaving as if under the effects of a *magic aura* spell.

At any point thereafter, the owner of the *book of written whispers* can write a message on the source page. This message can be up to 25 words long, a simple line drawing, or even a straightforward map. When the book's owner writes the activation word in the page's margin (this word does not count against the message's total word count), the message or image inscribed on the page instantly duplicates on the page's linked secret letter, and the actual contents of both the source page and the secret letter are hidden by a *secret page* effect. The carrier of the secret letter can use the activation word to reveal the actual contents of the message or to restore the misleading secret page contents.

As a standard action, the owner of a *book of written whispers* can rip an entire source page out of the book. Doing so causes its linked secret letter to crumble to ash, whether or not any messages have yet been sent. A *book of written whispers* can be used only 25 times before it is filled; once used, a page cannot be reused to send a new message.

CONSTRUCTION REQUIREMENTS	COST 3,000 GP

Craft Wondrous Item, *magic aura*, *secret page*, *sending*

Prime Conspirator Rogue Talent

From phrases and tips found in "Prime Conspirator," enterprising rogues have developed the following deciphering technique.

Expert Cipher (Ex): A rogue with this ability can attempt a Linguistics check to decipher a single page of text as a full-round action instead of taking 1 minute as normal. In addition, when the rogue attempts a Use Magic Device check to cast a spell from a scroll, she is treated as though she had the minimum score in the appropriate ability score to cast that spell. Finally, the rogue can choose to add her Intelligence modifier to her Use Magic Device skill checks instead of her Charisma modifier.

Prime Gallant, The Drunken Hero

Cayden Cailean stumbled into the Starstone Cathedral on a drunken wager. Three days later he emerged profoundly changed in some ways and remarkably unchanged in others. While he had undeniably ascended to godhood, he continued acting much as he had before, fighting for worthy causes of his own choosing regardless of the odds. *The Majestic Book of the Prime Ascended* praises Cayden Cailean for his bravery in the face of danger and his bold devotion to freedom, both in his opposition to slavery and in his own code of conduct. The "Prime Gallant" chapter encourages mortals to follow Cayden Cailean's example, overcoming their fear to pursue the course of action they feel is correct, regardless of the personal consequences. It is no surprise that the chapter is wildly popular in Andoran, but the text has also found a surprising amount of acclaim in the pirate enclaves of the Shackles and the people of the River Kingdoms—two places where bravery and the ability to quickly make and follow through on risky decisions are valued.

Prime Gallant Feats

Much of the contents of "Prime Gallant" focus on techniques of bravado that allow fighters to use their bravery class feature in new ways.

Bravery in Action

Sometimes the key to bravery is acting before you have time to be scared.

Prerequisites: Bravery class feature, worshiper of Cayden Cailean.

Benefit: You can add the bonus from bravery to your initiative checks.

UNBOUND BRAVERY

Your firm dedication to the principles of courage and freedom allows you to escape your bonds more easily.

Prerequisites: Bravery class feature, worshiper of Cayden Cailean.

Benefit: You can add the bonus from bravery to Escape Artist checks and combat maneuver checks to escape a grapple. If your bonus from bravery is +2 or higher, then once per day, you can grant that bonus to an ally within 30 feet on a Will save against a fear effect, an Escape Artist check, or a combat maneuver check to escape a grapple. Granting this bonus to an ally is an immediate action and must be declared before the result of your ally's check is revealed.

UNDAUNTED BRAVERY

It takes more than the average threat to intimidate you, and you've mastered the art of menacing your foes by implying violence through your cheerful smile.

Prerequisites: Bravery class feature, worshiper of Cayden Cailean.

Benefit: You can add your bonus from bravery to Intimidate checks and to the DC to intimidate you.

PRIME GALLANT MAGIC ITEM

Inspired by Cayden's courage, "Prime Gallant" contains directions for the creation of an amulet that protects its wearer against fear.

AMULET OF COURAGE		PRICE 6,000 GP
SLOT neck	**CL** 3rd	**WEIGHT** —
AURA faint abjuration		

These amulets are fashioned of finely worked silver and depict an overflowing tankard. Once per day, when the wearer of an *amulet of courage* is affected by a magical or supernatural fear effect, the amulet casts *remove fear* on the wearer. In addition, if the wearer of the amulet has the bravery class feature, she increases the bonus she receives on Will saves against fear by 1.

CONSTRUCTION REQUIREMENTS	COST 2,500 GP

Craft Wondrous Items, *remove fear*

PRIME SCHOLAR, MASTER OF MASTERS

Irori, Master of Masters, ascended to godhood with no external assistance. He achieved his state of divinity through rigorous self-perfection of mind, body, and spirit. Many texts and works of art focus on Irori's physical achievements as a supreme martial artist, exemplifying his aspect of the god of self-perfection. *The Majestic Book of the Prime Ascended* instead praises Irori's mental perfection through his concerns of history and knowledge. The chapter encourages self-tutelage by studying a myriad of academic subjects. "Prime Scholar" has found its greatest popularity within the Inner Sea region of Jalmeray, but is also in known in Absalom, Osirion, Qadira, and other areas where worship of Irori is common. Most followers of the Master of Masters consider the *Majestic Book of the Prime Ascended* to be secondary in importance to *Unbinding the Fetters*, but still value it for its numerous insights. Curiously, the bulk of the techniques in "Prime Scholar" are of use to bards, not monks. The bardic masterpieces outlined below focus on helping others improve the body, mind, or spirit, the three foundations of Irori's teaching. Rules for bardic masterpieces appear on page 21 of *Pathfinder RPG Ultimate Magic*.

EXHILARATING PRAYER OF GRACE (DANCE)

You lead your audience through a series of stretches and exercises designed to warm the muscles and increase blood circulation.

Prerequisite: Perform (dance) 4 ranks.

Cost: Feat or 2nd-level bard spell known.

Effect: After completing the series of exercises, anyone who observed the performance (including yourself) gains a circumstance bonus on all Acrobatics checks and to CMD equal to 1/5 of your bard level (minimum +1). This bonus persists for 10 minutes.

Use: 1 round of bardic performance.

Action: 3 rounds.

HYMN OF RESTORATIVE HARMONICS (SING, WIND)

You perform a song of such beauty that it touches the soul of any who hear it, allowing them to recover from any adverse conditions.

Prerequisite: Perform (sing) or Perform (wind) 6 ranks.

Cost: Feat or 3rd-level bard spell known.

Effect: At the end of the round on which you complete this song, all allies within 30 feet who observed your performance gain a new saving throw to end the ongoing effects of certain debilitating conditions. An ally who is exhausted, fatigued, nauseated, sickened, staggered, or stunned as the result of a previously failed saving throw can attempt a new saving throw to immediately end one of the above effects. Characters under multiple effects must choose which effect they wish to attempt to end prematurely. Effects that did not grant a save to resist (such as the stun effect of *power word stun*) can't be ended by this masterpiece.

In addition, anyone who observed this performance gains the effects of *delay poison* at a caster level equal to your bard level.

Use: 3 bardic performance rounds.

Action: 1 full round.

STIRRING DISCOURSE OF THE MIND (ORATORY)

You lecture your audience on the merits of studious endeavors and inspire them with new insights into the subject matter. As a result of your discourse, those who listen become more receptive to knowledge.

Prerequisite: Perform (oratory) 4 ranks.

Cost: Feat or 2nd-level bard spell known.

Effect: Upon completion of your lecture, anyone who listened to your performance gains a +4 insight bonus on Knowledge checks to perform research in a library, and on Spellcraft checks to identify the properties of magic items. This bonus lasts for 10 minutes.

Use: 2 rounds of bardic performance.

Action: 1 minute.

TRAITS OF THE PRIME ASCENDED

Copies of *The Majestic Book of the Prime Ascended* can be found throughout the Inner Sea region and beyond, and those who follow its teachings can begin learning from the lessons it contains early in life. Listed below are several traits that characters could begin play with, if they grew up in areas where the book's teachings were popular. While the tome itself focuses on five specific ascended deities, these traits can be selected by anyone, for their teachings are not tied to specific deities as much as they are to the ideals of ascension itself.

Apprentice (Faith): During your studies of *The Majestic Book of the Prime Ascended*, you learned some minor magical tricks. Select a single 0-level spell from the sorcerer/wizard spell list. You can cast this spell 1 time per day as a spell-like ability.

Arcane Scholar (Faith): Study of the "Prime Archmage" chapter has broadened your magical knowledge. Choose either Knowledge (arcana) or Spellcraft; you gain a +1 trait bonus on that skill and it is a class skill for you.

Crusader (Faith): From studying "Prime Commander" and reading accounts of the battles in the Worldwound, you have trained to be a crusader against demonic forces. You gain a +1 trait bonus on attack rolls against outsiders with the chaotic subtype.

Masked (Faith): You learned from "Prime Conspirator" that keeping secrets often means hiding your true identity. Once per day, when attempting a Disguise check, roll twice and take the better result.

Secret Keeper (Faith): Avoiding inquisitors and agents of your enemies has required you to become a practiced liar. You gain a +3 trait bonus on Bluff checks when they are opposed by another's Sense Motive check.

Student of History (Faith): One can move toward enlightenment by understanding the mistakes of past generations. You gain a +1 trait bonus on Knowledge (history) checks, and Knowledge (history) is a class skill for you.

Traditionalist (Faith): You attempt to maintain older traditions despite changing social norms, and find great value in the trappings and codes of the aristocracy. You gain a +1 trait bonus on Knowledge (nobility) checks, and Knowledge (nobility) is a class skill for you.

Undaunted (Faith): Following the path of freedom has resulted in you being threatened by ruffians and bullies throughout your childhood, and it now takes a lot to rattle you. You increase the DC to demoralize you with an Intimidate check by 2.

Unshackled (Faith): You have escaped slavery or other imprisonment and have vowed never to be shackled again. You gain a +1 trait bonus on Escape Artist checks, and Escape Artist is a class skill for you.

Untrained Scholar (Faith): While scholarship is not your primary focus, you have spent enough time in classrooms and libraries to learn a few things. Once per day, you can attempt a Knowledge (geography), Knowledge (history) or Knowledge (local) check untrained with a +2 trait bonus.

Meditations and Revelations

Amvirak Twin-Souls, born as Amvirak Doleres, spent much of his life as an outspoken critic of all things divine, and frequently went to extreme lengths in his crusade to enforce his views upon the devout. Lord of a minor province in northern Taldor and an accomplished wizard, Amvirak would seek out clerics, monks, oracles, and other devout or outspoken worshipers. He imprisoned those he could capture in cells below his manor and subjected them to a series of grisly secular inquisitions wherein the faithful were submitted to grim tortures, taunts that their deity had forsaken them, and claims that their faith was worthless. Those who eventually renounced their religion Amvirak released, but those who persevered he kept imprisoned in his dungeons for years, or even decades.

Late in his life, though, the cruel Lord Amvirak experienced a powerful spiritual awakening when one of his prisoners, a priest of Sarenrae, managed what the others had not. He turned Amvirak's arguments back against him, forgave him, and redeemed him. The nature of what this nameless priest said to Amvirak is unknown—but the effects were swift. Amvirak released his prisoners and sold everything he owned, splitting the proceeds of the sale among his surviving victims. He then accompanied the priest of Sarenrae back to Qadira, where he spent the rest of his days in seclusion in a remote monastery. He took the name "Twin-Souls" at this time, claiming that his old, tainted soul had been stripped from him and a fresh new one had been granted in its place.

Amvirak lived the rest of his days in that monastery, where he worked off the spiritual debt he'd incurred in his persecution of the divine. He penned many lengthy works about his experiences, and while the earlier ones wallowed in self-pity and remorse, Amvirak's observations on faith grew more astute as his own devotion grew. He never accepted Sarenrae as his patron deity (although he certainly admired her), instead spending his time seeking a way to help others learn that faith was not a crutch or a flaw but a great source of strength worthy of pursuing. His final treatise was the lengthy tome for which he is most well-known: *Meditations and Revelations*.

The pages of this tome outline Amvirak's spiritual awakening, but not a trace of his earlier self-pity and shame is apparent in the text. He records nine revelations that he received from the divine, as well as a number of essays on meditation techniques and the power and importance of prayer and worship. The book is not specific to any one god, and while the religions of many different deities find it to be useful, it is generally considered secondary reading material. Those that value it most generally do so for its meditative techniques, rather than its philosophy.

Faith Traits

Meditations and Revelations enjoys widespread distribution, though not necessarily popularity, in the Inner Sea, Vudra, Tian Xia, and beyond. The methods and techniques detailed within are highly subjective, and two different readers can easily come away with two entirely distinct but equally effective interpretation. In certain regions where the book has gained traction among the faithful, their careful study and exegesis of the book's contents have resulted in the development of unique traits that can guide one's mind. A character need not hail from any one of these source regions to select one of the following faith traits, but should have an opportunity in her background to have studied the wisdom of *Meditations and Revelations*, either directly or through the guidance of a learned mentor.

Jalmeray

The meditative techniques described in the book are particularly valued by the monasteries on the isle of Jalmeray, and many of the isle's devout have incorporated these techniques into their training. While many of these techniques were first developed ages ago in the distant land of Vudra, they are not constrained to Jalmeray, and the methods are spreading quickly throughout the Inner Sea region, particularly through the nearby lands of Qadira, Osirion, and Katapesh.

Heedful Readiness (Faith): Your years of meditation and mindfulness allow you to act correctly on a moment's notice. Once per day, you can add your Wisdom modifier to an initiative check.

Kyonin

Many elves appreciate the meditative techniques found in *Meditations and Revelations*, though those who pursue them generally do so less for self-improvement and more to find peace, tranquility, and mindfulness. A handful of very devoted readers from Kyonin have even discovered a way to augment sleep with meditation so as to make the daily ritual of spell preparation flow even more smoothly.

Meditative Rest (Faith): When you rest, you ignore the first time you are interrupted during that rest for the purposes of determining how long you need to rest in full to regain the capacity to regain spells, provided the interruption lasts no more than 15 minutes. If you cast spells during this interruption, you don't count these against your daily limit of spells when you wake and prepare spells.

NIDAL

The Umbral Court takes a dim view of *Meditations and Revelations*, whose hopeful message and spiritual affirmations lend strength and comfort to the Desnans who defy the government's oppressive regime. Ownership of the book has been outlawed, with the penalties for being caught with a copy ranging from torture to death, yet those who would fight against the Umbral Court find much within the pages to bolster their cause.

Darkest Before Dawn (Faith): Your devotion sustains you when others would fall to despair. You gain a +2 trait bonus on saving throws against spells with the emotion[UM], fear, or pain[UM] descriptor. Once per day, you can increase this bonus to +4 for a single save, but you must make this decision before you attempt the saving throw.

RAZMIRAN

Unsurprisingly, the priests of Razmir have little love for *Meditations and Revelations*, as its message lies in the power of faith itself (and otherwise blends poorly with their doctrines). The church of Razmir distributes a heavily edited and altered version of the book that lacks most of the meditative techniques. What remains has been reworked to focus on Razmir as the only god worthy of worship, but these new techniques have inspired a certain strength in the faithful of Razmir who take the revised book to heart.

Strength of Submission (Faith): Your faith in the church of Razmir and willingness to surrender yourself to him lend you strength and clarity. Whenever you are under the effects of a compulsion effect, you gain a +1 trait bonus on attack and damage rolls.

FEATS

Meditations and Revelations contains extensive instruction on the importance of opening the mind and soul to one's deity, and in so doing achieving spiritual communion and harmony. The following feats are commonly taken by those who follow the book's teachings.

DIVERSE OBEDIENCE

Your intense faith in your deity allows you to gain boons not granted to most followers.

Prerequisites: Deific Obedience[ISG], Knowledge (religion) 5 ranks, alignment must match that of your worshiped deity.

Benefit: You are treated as though you had 2 more Hit Dice than you actually do for the purposes of determining what divine boons you gain as a result of performing your deity's obedience. Diverse Obedience doesn't allow access to divine boons granted through prestige classes early, as those boons are tied to prestige class levels gained, not overall Hit Dice. If you take levels in a prestige class or archetype that offers accelerated access to a boon, this benefit may be superfluous.

Additionally, whenever you would gain a boon as a result of your Deific Obedience feat (and not through a prestige class), you can choose among the options available for evangelist, exalted, or sentinel boons. Once you make the selection, it is permanent, but you can choose from a different category each time you gain a new boon as you increase your Hit Dice.

DIVINE COMMUNION

Your close, personal connection with your deity grants you insight into his or her wishes.

Prerequisites: Wisdom 13, alignment must match that of your worshiped deity.

Benefit: Once per day as a swift action, you can ponder whether or not your deity would approve or disapprove of a particular course of action, and whether that action would impact your alignment. The GM decides if the action is one your deity would approve of, and if it is, you gain an insight bonus equal to your Wisdom modifier (minimum of +1) on any d20 roll made in association with that action during this round. For every 3 ranks you have in Knowledge (religion), you can use this ability an additional time per day, to a maximum of 6 times a day.

MINOR MIRACLE

You can call upon your deity for a minor miracle.

Prerequisites: Wis 12, Knowledge (religion) 5 ranks, alignment must match that of your worshiped deity.

Benefit: Choose two domains associated with your deity (if you have access to one or more domains already, the chosen domains can be the same ones you already have access to, or different ones). Once per day, by presenting a holy symbol of your deity and calling out in supplication, you can cast the 1st-level spell associated with either of the two chosen domains as a spell-like ability. You choose which domain's spell you cast at the time you use the ability. Your caster level for this effect is equal to your total Hit Dice, and the saving throw DC, if any, is Charisma-based.

REWARD OF THE FAITHFUL

Your intense belief in your deity allows you to benefit more from divine magic he or she provides.

Prerequisites: Knowledge (religion) 1 rank, alignment must match that of your worshiped deity.

Benefit: Whenever you are the only target of a divine spell cast by a follower of your chosen deity other than you, the spell's caster level is treated as though it were 2 higher than it actually is. Additionally, whenever you regain hit points as a result of a worshiper of your deity other than you channeling energy or casting a cure spell, you regain 1 additional hit point per die rolled for the healing gained.

MEDITATIVE SPELLS

The following spells appear in *Meditations and Revelations*, but beyond that are noteworthy in the ways that they combine traditional spellcasting with deep meditative techniques. These meditative spells fall into an unusual category and share the "meditative" descriptor. Meditative spells are not cast like other spells—they are cast during the period of the day when a spellcaster prepares her spells. A meditative spell must already be prepared at the time when you start your 1-hour spell preparation ritual, and at the end of that time, the meditative spell of your choosing is cast, leaving you with that one spell slot used for the remainder of the day. You can have only one meditative spell in effect on you at any one time. All meditative spells have a range of personal and a target of you, and they can't be brewed into potions or part of similar one-use items like elixirs. A meditative spell can be placed on a scroll or in a wand, but the act of casting the spell must always be incorporated into the user's spell-preparation time; it also takes 1 hour for a character who succeeds at an appropriate Use Magic Device check to operate such an item.

Though some of these spells are on the cleric spell list, they can't be part of an oracle's list of spells known. Spontaneous casters such as oracles or sorcerers cannot benefit from the effects of a meditative spell, nor can characters who use such magic without preparation via Use Magic Device and a magic item, since part of the process of casting and maintaining the effects of a meditative spell involves tying the act of weaving the magic into the very process of meditation and study that a prepared spellcaster (such as a cleric or wizard) undergoes at the start of every day.

ENLIGHTENED STEP

School transmutation [air, meditative]; **Level** cleric 6, druid 6, shaman 6
Casting Time 1 hour
Components V, M (soothing incense worth 600 gp)
Range personal
Target you
Duration 24 hours or until discharged

Through careful regulation of your body's mystical energies, thoughtful control of your poise and balance, and the focus in your mind on the surety of each and every step you take, you are able to make your steps lighter than air. This grants you the benefits of *air walk*, except as noted above. Additionally, at any time during the spell's duration, you can expend the spell's remaining duration as a swift action in order to gain a fly speed of 120 feet with perfect maneuverability for 1 minute. After this time, the spell ends.

FIREWALKER'S MEDITATION

School abjuration [meditative]; **Level** cleric 4, druid 4, paladin 3, shaman 4, wizard 4
Casting Time 1 hour
Components V, M (soothing incense worth 400 gp)
Range personal
Target you
Duration 24 hours or until discharged

You focus your mind on blocking out pain, allowing your body to endure punishments that would be otherwise unbearable. While under the effects of this spell, you continue to register pain—you simply don't suffer the deleterious effects such sensations bring. For example, if you were lit on fire as you slept, you would still wake from the pain of burning even though some of the fire damage you endured (perhaps all of it) would be negated by this spell.

You gain DR 5/magic, resist fire 10, and a +4 bonus on saving throws to resist pain effects. Once the spell has prevented a total of 10 points of damage per caster level (maximum 100 points), it is discharged. At any time during the spell's duration when you take damage that would be subject to the damage reduction or energy resistance granted by this spell, you can expend the spell's remaining duration as an immediate action in order to increase the effects to DR 10/magic, resist fire 30, and immunity to pain effects. If you do so, these enhanced effects persist for 3 rounds. After this time, the spell ends.

RITE OF BODILY PURITY

School abjuration [meditative]; **Level** cleric 1, druid 1, paladin 1, ranger 1, shaman 1
Casting Time 1 hour
Components V, M (soothing incense worth 100 gp)
Range personal
Target you
Duration 24 hours or until discharged

You energize your body's immune system, improving your ability to resist toxins and ailments. You gain a +2 resistance bonus on saving throws to resist diseases, drugs, and poisons. Additionally, at any time during the spell's duration, whenever you fail a saving throw to resist a disease, drug, or poison, you can expend the spell's remaining duration as an immediate action in order to reroll that saving throw. You must take the second result, even if it's worse. The +2 resistance bonus granted by the spell applies to the reroll, but after you make this reroll, the spell ends.

RITE OF CENTERED MIND

School abjuration [meditative]; **Level** cleric 1, druid 1, shaman 1, wizard 1
Casting Time 1 hour
Components V, M (soothing incense worth 100 gp)
Range personal
Target you
Duration 24 hours or until discharged

You heighten your awareness of your own thoughts, allowing you to more easily resist outside influences. You gain a +1 resistance bonus on saving throws to resist mind-affecting effects. This resistance bonus is increased to +2 if the effect is an emotion or fear effect. Additionally, at any time during the spell's duration, whenever you fail a saving throw to resist a mind-affecting effect, you can expend the spell's remaining duration as an immediate action in order to reroll that saving throw. You must take the second result, even if it's worse. The +2 resistance bonus granted by the spell applies to the reroll, but after you make this reroll, the spell ends.

SEE BEYOND

School divination [meditative]; **Level** cleric 3, shaman 3, witch 3, wizard 3
Casting Time 1 hour
Components V, M (soothing incense worth 300 gp)
Range personal
Target you
Duration 24 hours or until discharged

You attune your mind and your sight to the hidden world of spirits. You gain a +5 circumstance bonus on Perception checks; this circumstance bonus increases to a +10 circumstance bonus on Perception checks to find invisible creatures or objects, incorporeal creatures or objects, or things that exist only on the Ethereal Plane. Additionally, at any time during the spell's duration, you can push your ethereal vision even further as a swift action. When you do, you can see through solid objects (as if using a *ring of x-ray vision*) for 5 rounds. After this time, the spell ends.

SPIRIT BONDS

School divination [meditative]; **Level** cleric 3, shaman 3, witch 3, wizard 3
Casting Time 1 hour
Components V, M (soothing incense worth 300 gp)
Range personal
Target you; see text
Duration 24 hours or until discharged

You heighten your awareness of up to one willing creature or object per 3 caster levels, each of which must be within 30 feet of you during the entire hour you spend preparing spells and casting *spirit bonds*. By concentrating on one of these creatures or objects as a full-round action, you can learn its direction and relative distance from your location, provided that it is on the same plane. In the case of a creature, you can also learn the state of its emotion or health aura as a full-round action (see page 198 of *Pathfinder RPG Occult Adventures* for more information about auras). In the case of an object, you can also get a sense of how damaged it is, similar to reading the health aura of a creature, or, in the case of a magic item that must be activated, you can learn when it was last activated (a full-round action in either case).

Additionally, at any time during the spell's duration, you can deliver a single message to any of the creatures that participated in the spell. This message is delivered telepathically regardless of range and can be up to 25 words in length. Delivering a message in this way severs your connection with that character, and you can no longer learn information about that creature through this spell, but doing so does not impact the remaining duration you have linked to other creatures or objects.

VISUALIZATION OF THE BODY

School transmutation [meditative]; **Level** cleric 2, druid 2, magus 2, ranger 2, shaman 2, wizard 2
Casting Time 1 hour
Components V, M (soothing incense worth 200 gp)
Range personal
Target you
Duration 24 hours or until discharged

You focus your mind on one aspect of your body, aligning the energies within your body to enhance that element. Choose a single physical ability score (Constitution, Dexterity, or Strength). If you choose Strength or Dexterity, you gain a +5 bonus on skill checks associated with that ability score. If you choose Constitution, your maximum and current hit points increase by an amount equal to your Hit Dice.

At any time during the spell's duration, you can expend the spell's remaining duration as an immediate action in order to gain a one-time physical enhancement associated with the

ability score you chose to visualize, as detailed below. After you do so, the spell ends.

Constitution: You immediately regain a number of hit points equal to 1d8 + your total character level.

Dexterity: You gain a +4 dodge bonus to your Armor Class for 3 rounds.

Strength: You gain a +6 bonus on all Strength checks to break objects and on checks to escape or establish grapples for 1 minute.

VISUALIZATION OF THE MIND

School transmutation [meditative]; **Level** cleric 2, shaman 2, wizard 2

Casting Time 1 hour

Components V, M (soothing incense worth 200 gp)

Range personal

Target you

Duration 24 hours or until discharged

You enhance a single aspect of your mind, nurturing and empowering it. Choose a single mental ability score (Charisma, Intelligence, or Wisdom). You gain a +5 bonus on ability checks and skill checks associated with that ability score.

At any time during the spell's duration, you can expend the spell's remaining duration as an immediate action in order to gain a one-time mental enhancement associated with the ability score you chose to visualize, as detailed below. After you do so, the spell ends.

Charisma: You are immediately infused with a wave of supernatural luck, and gain a +2 luck bonus on all d20 rolls for 1 minute.

Intelligence: You immediately gain a flash of insight, and gain a number of ranks equal to your Hit Dice in any skill in which you have no ranks. These ranks last for 1 minute, during which time you can also treat that skill as a class skill.

Wisdom: When you fail a Will save, you can immediately attempt that saving throw again, gaining a +4 bonus on the new saving throw to resist the effect.

OBEDIENT ARCHETYPES

The following archetypes are often taken by those who have studied from *Meditations and Revelations* and taken its message to heart. Both archetypes require the character to perform regular obediences to her chosen deity, just as one must to gain the benefits of the Divine Obedience feat. These obediences are identical to those required by Divine Obedience—for religions that do not have official obediences printed, you can either work with your GM to create appropriate obediences or simply assume that the obedience in question is something relatively minor that your character can take care of during your spell preparation ritual. Failure to follow this daily obedience causes you to lose all of the abilities granted by your chosen archetype. In this event, you do not regain the abilities you altered or replaced via the archetype—you simply lose access to that element of power granted until you next perform the obedience.

For more information on obediences, see pages 10 and 210 of *Pathfinder Campaign Setting: Inner Sea Gods*.

DIVINE CHAMPION (WARPRIEST ARCHETYPE)

Divine champions are unswervingly devoted to their causes, and specialize in bringing battle to the enemies of their faiths. They are similar to divine paragons in many ways, but tend to focus more on their deity's combat prowess rather than seeking to become a physical manifestation of the deity's will.

Devotion: A divine champion's power comes from his close connection to his deity. He must worship a deity, and must maintain the same alignment as that deity.

Obedient Champion: At 3rd level, the divine champion gains Deific Obedience[ISG] as a bonus feat, even if he doesn't meet the feat's prerequisites. When a divine champion gains boons from this feat, he gains the appropriate sentinel boon offered by his deity, rather than gaining the exalted boon.

This replaces the bonus feat gained at 3rd level.

Know the Infidel (Ex): At 6th level, the divine champion becomes an expert at combating enemies of his faith. He must choose a deity whose alignment is opposed to his own deity's alignment in at least one way (good versus evil or law versus chaos); preferably, he should choose a deity whose alignment diametrically opposes that of his own deity. If the divine champion worships a deity whose alignment is neutral, he must instead select a deity whose alignment is chaotic evil, chaotic good, lawful evil, or lawful good. The choice of this enemy deity is subject to GM approval. At the GM's discretion, the divine champion may be allowed to choose a philosophy or religious organization that's not affiliated with a deity, such as the Green Faith, the Pure Legion, or the Whispering Way, but only if that philosophy or religious organization is an enemy of the divine champion's deity. The divine champion gains a +2 bonus on Bluff, Intimidate, Knowledge, Perception, and Sense Motive checks against followers of the enemy faith, as well as a +2 bonus on weapon attack and damage rolls made against them. Additionally, he can attempt Knowledge skill checks relating to the deity and its church untrained, even if the DC is higher than 10.

Every 6 paladin levels thereafter (12th and 18th level), the divine champion can select an additional deity to oppose. In addition, at each such interval, the bonus against the followers of any one deity he selected previously (including the one just selected, if so desired) increases by +2.

This replaces the bonus feats gained at 6th, 12th, and 18th levels.

Fervent Boon (Sp): Beginning at 9th level, a divine champion can call upon his deity for minor boons. By expending one or more uses of his fervor ability, he can cast one of the spell-like abilities included in his deity's first sentinel boon. By expending one use of fervor, he can cast the spell-like ability that the boon normally grants three uses of per day; by expending two uses of fervor he can cast the spell-like ability that the boon normally grants twice per day; and by expending three uses of fervor, he can cast the spell-like ability that the boon normally grants once per day. These uses don't count against any uses granted by the boon.

This replaces the bonus feat gained at 9th level.

DIVINE PARAGON (CLERIC ARCHETYPE)

Divine paragons strive to emulate their god's ideals as closely as possible. They might see themselves as an incarnation of their deity in the flesh, or they could simply seek to embody the physical and spiritual ideals set forth by their deity. Many divine paragons go as far as to alter their appearance, as best as possible, to look similar to their chosen deity, but such a level of devotion is not required by the archetype.

Devoted Domain: A divine paragon is intensely devoted to a single deity, and her alignment must be identical to her deity's alignment. She gains Deific Obedience[ISG] as a bonus feat, even if she doesn't meet the feat's prerequisites. She gains access to her boons at an accelerated rate (see below) rather than the standard HD-based rate granted by Deific Obedience (and as such cannot benefit from the accelerated rate granted by the Diverse Obedience feat).

When the divine paragon selects her domains, she must designate one of the two domains she gains as her devoted domain. She gains all of this domain's granted powers and domain spells normally. For her other domain, she gains only its domain spells—she does not gain any of the granted powers of that domain. Instead, she must choose from the evangelist, exalted, or sentinel boons granted by her deity (as detailed in *Pathfinder Campaign Setting: Inner Sea Gods*). At 5th level, she gains access to the first boon granted by her deity. At 11th level, she gains access to the second boon. At 14th level, she gains access to the third boon.

In order to retain access to her domain spells, the domain powers of her devoted domain, and the boons granted by Deific Obedience, the divine paragon must perform her obedience daily. If she fails to do so, she loses access to these abilities until she next performs her obedience (but she can still cast spells, channel energy, and perform other abilities granted by her cleric levels).

This ability alters domains.

Divine Brand (Ex): At 1st level, a mark appears somewhere on the divine paragon's body. The mark's location varies by individual and faith, but takes the form of the deity's holy symbol and generally appears in a location easy to display, such as on the hand, forearm, chest, or face. An uncovered divine brand functions as a holy (or unholy) symbol and as a divine focus for spellcasting. The divine paragon's aura is even more powerful than a typical cleric's as a result of her devotion, and her cleric level is treated as 1 higher for the purpose of determining the strength of her aura when it is viewed by spells like *detect good*.

This ability alters aura.

On Virtue

On Virtue is a work comparing paladins' religions and codes, compiled from the holy texts of numerous lawful or good deities and demigods worshiped across Golarion. Keleshite paladins generated the oldest-known copies during the Age of Glory, when these crusaders sought to detail the vast array of good-aligned entities that had whispered in their dreams or inspired them while they were deep in meditation. After it was first published, dwarven priests who found much in the writings akin to their own beliefs significantly expanded the text. *On Virtue* has since become one of the few popular religious texts in the Five Kings Mountains to depict deities whose worshipers are largely non-dwarves.

Due to the quality and variety of the material, *On Virtue* became acclaimed among paladins in many different regions, but ironically also served as a handbook for hunting the servants of good-aligned deities in places such Geb and Rahadoum. In these nations hostile to paladins, *On Virtue* is banned and only established paladin hunters are allowed to keep copies of the book—to better know the enemy.

Modern copies of *On Virtue* vary slightly in their contents according to the interests of those reprinting it, with the most complete and consistent version printed in Tar-Kazmukh in the Five Kings Mountains. It is also widely circulated among the crusaders of Mendev and the knights of Lastwall, and in the Tempering Hall in Absalom.

Although all paladins must be lawful good, the specifics of their codes of conduct vary according to the agendas and standards of their patron deities and individuals' interpretation of their deities' mandates and teachings. Below are sample codes and character traits that a holy warrior of each faith would follow, as recorded in *On Virtue*. While these traits and codes are most likely to be taken by paladins, they are not limited to this class, and any lawful good characters seeking to uphold the faith of one of these deities can use these resources to bolster their cause.

Each of the faiths detailed below is presented with two unique religion traits that worshipers of that deity can take, regardless of whether or not the character in question is a divine spellcaster.

Andoletta

Andoletta, an empyreal lord and ruler of the fourth layer of Heaven, is the patron of consolation, respect, and security. She is also known as Grandmother Crow. Her worshipers are authority figures (especially teachers and judges), the bereaved, and the elderly.

Andoletta's Consolation (Andoletta): You had a close encounter with a servant or worshiper of Andoletta who provided you with a memorable, if unconventional, consolation after a loss. As a result, you gain a +2 trait bonus on saving throws against emotion and fear effects. If you are immune to fear, you instead gain a +4 trait bonus on saves against emotion effects.

Enemy of Delusion (Andoletta): You were once faced with a grave injustice committed by an ignorant or delusional person, and righteous indignation moved you to correct the mistaken party. Once per day, when you confirm a critical hit against, successfully use a smite attack on, or use lay on hands on a creature that is affected by a charm or compulsion effect, you can invoke Andoletta to open the target's eyes. If the effect originally allowed a saving throw to resist it, the target can attempt a new saving throw against the charm or compulsion; if she's successful, the the effect ends immediately.

Andoletta's Paladin Code

Andoletta's paladins serve courts and other authorities. They seek to protect innocence and dispel foolishness. Their tenets include the following affirmations.

- Children must be nurtured lest their innocence become callousness or ignorance. I will never be cold or negligent to a child.
- Virtue relies upon wisdom, and wisdom relies upon true awareness. I will never leave a falsehood unchallenged.
- I will be firm with the ignorant, but not cruel. Ignorance can be corrected.
- I will respect my elders' knowledge and wisdom, but won't abide the spreading of complacency or ignorance.

Angradd

The youngest of Torag's brothers, Angradd the Forge-Fire is a dwarven deity of fire, tradition, and war. He and his older brother Magrim work together to decide the fates of dwarven spirits. Angradd represents those souls who demonstrate valor, courage, and keen tactical acumen. His worshipers aspire to be righteous enough to earn a place of honor alongside Angradd.

Angradd's Valor (Angradd): You hope to earn a place at Angradd's side after death and are inspired to charge with all your might into any righteous battle. You gain a +1 trait bonus on all melee attack rolls when you charge.

Rousing Courage (Angradd): A dwarven warrior's simple act of courage in Angradd's name inspired you during one of your first battles. Now, you strive to be equally inspiring to others. Once per day, when you generate an effect that grants a morale bonus, increase that bonus by 1 for all creatures affected.

Angradd's Paladin Code

The paladins of Angradd are tacticians and commanders. Their tenets include the following affirmations.

- Passivity gives evil a chance to thrive and spread. I will proactively seek out villains to thwart.
- Traditions make us who we are. I will uphold the traditions of my people.
- War is a dangerous tool. I will gladly risk myself for a worthy cause but will never promote pointless war.
- Valor requires judgment. I will use the knowledge and the resources at my disposal to avoid needless loss of life.

Arqueros

Arqueros, the Golden Bulwark, is the empyreal lord of bodyguards, protection, and watchfulness.

Eye of Arqueros (Arqueros): You once fell asleep during a task that required your attention. A vision of Arqueros awakened you just in time to avoid failing at your task. You gain a +3 trait bonus on Perception checks attempted while you are alone on guard duty.

Living Bulwark (Arqueros): The Golden Bulwark inspires you to give your all for those you protect. Once per day, when an adjacent ally is targeted by an attack but before the attack roll is attempted, you can interpose yourself as an immediate action. You become the target of the attack instead.

Arqueros's Paladin Code

The paladins of Arqueros are defense-oriented generals and bodyguards of virtuous public figures and honorable clients. Their tenets include the following affirmations.

- I will never abandon an innocent in need of protection.
- The role of guardian is a sacred one. I will never neglect my duties when I agree to guard or protect others, even if they seem unworthy of my protection.
- A guardian is only as effective as his weapons and armor. I will maintain mine in peak condition at all times, repairing and cleaning them as consistently as possible without neglecting my charge.

Chaldira Zuzaristan

Chaldira Zuzaristan is a hero-deity of the halfling people and close friend of Desna. Her portfolio is battle, luck, and mischief. Also called the Calamitous Turn, Chaldira embodies halfling luck and the adventuring drive that makes it so very useful. Among the deities in *On Virtue*, she is the least standard and her paladins are the least common, yet her faith remains as staunch a foe of evil as any detailed in the tome.

Chaldira's Luck (Chaldira Zuzaristan): You found yourself in deep trouble in your youth but stumbled upon an unlikely way out after praying to Chaldira Zuzaristan

for luck. Once per day, you can roll twice and take the better result on a skill check.

Mischievous Smite (Chaldira Zuzaristan): You consider mischief a sacred rite in humbling enemies. You do not provoke attacks of opportunity when performing a dirty trick[APG] combat maneuver while your smite evil bonus applies to combat maneuver checks. If you already do not provoke such attacks of opportunity (such as by having Improved Dirty Trick[APG]), you instead gain a +2 trait bonus on dirty trick[APG] combat maneuver checks against creatures that are the targets of your smite.

Chaldira Zuzaristan's Paladin Code

The paladins of Chaldira are reckless champions of the downtrodden and ignored. Their tenets include the following affirmations.

- I will not let caution stay my hand in the face of evil.
- I will be relentless in serving my community.
- Every discovery might be an asset for good. Learning and exploration are my sacred duties.
- Levity deflates pride. I will never oppose good-natured mischief that violates no law.

Folgrit

Folgrit the Watchful Mother is the dwarven goddess of children, hearths, and mothers. She is Torag's wife, and does her best to keep his mind fresh when he worries or plans overmuch, challenging assumptions and reminding her husband of all he protects. She pays special attention to the families of those at war, widows, and orphans. Dwarven adoptive parents also pray to her.

Folgrit's Bounty (Folgrit): You were taught to tend the sacred hearth-fire and cook nourishing meals as a child. You gain a +1 trait bonus on Profession (cook) checks and can prepare a nourishing meal of up to eight portions with 1 hour of effort at a cost of 20 gp. Anyone who eats a portion within 1 day (which takes 10 minutes) gains a +1 morale bonus that can be applied to any one skill check or attack roll in the next 8 hours. The bonus must be applied before the roll is made and cannot be renewed by another meal for 1 day.

Folgrit's Mercy (Folgrit): You were called upon to defend your home or family at a vulnerable time and led with a clarity of mind you did not know you had. Once per day when you use lay on hands, you also cure the target of 1d4 points of Intelligence, Wisdom, or Charisma damage. You choose which ability score gains the healing effect.

Folgrit's Paladin Code

The paladins of Folgrit are protectors of home and hearth who safeguard sacred places in times of war and peace. Many are mothers who seek to help and protect children and other mothers. Their tenets include the following affirmations.

- Children are true innocents. I will protect them from harm above all else.

- A child's spirit is the light of a people. I will nurture children under my care.
- My home, whatever it might be, is always a refuge for the homeless.
- A clear mind is vital for any leader. I will never impair my judgment.
- I will always make time to help others learn and think clearly.

Kols

Kols the Oathkeeper is the dwarven demigod of duty, honor, and promises. When not attending to his father Torag or protecting his brother Grundinnar and sister Bolka, he punishes oathbreakers and those who neglect their duties.

Oathkeeper's Vow (Kols): The clergy of Kols trained you to make unbreakable vows. You add the following spells to the paladin spell list at the indicated levels: *command* (1st), *forbid action*[APG] (1st), *suggestion* (to fulfill a prior promise only; 2nd), *lesser geas* (3rd), *geas/quest* (4th).

Relentless Duty (Kols): You were raised with the mantra that fulfilling your duty must always come first. Now living up to a promise comes as easily as breathing. Once per day, you can take 10 on a skill check attempted as part of fulfilling a prior promise even if you are distracted or in combat.

Kols's Paladin Code

The paladins of Kols are skyseekers, honorable servants of rightful dwarven lords, steadfast guardians of dwarven sites, and punishers of deserters and oathbreakers. Their tenets include the following affirmations.

- My responsibilities to my people are a sacred duty to my god. I will never willingly shirk my duties.
- Oathbreakers and deserters undermine the bonds that hold society together. I will never allow one to go unpunished if it is within my power.
- A promise is sacred. I will never willingly break any oath or contract.

Ragathiel

Ragathiel is the empyreal lord of chivalry, duty, and vengeance. A child of the archdevil Dispater, Ragathiel turned away from evil and earned a place among the empyreal lords thanks to his tenacity and valor—traits he demands of his worshipers.

Avowed Inspiration (Ragathiel): In emulation of the empyreal lord's intensely channeled rage, you are an inspiration on the battlefield. Once per day, when you attack a foe who injured you during the same combat, you can inspire allies who can see you as a move action. Each other ally within 30 feet who can see you gains a +2 morale bonus on her next attack roll.

Redeemed by Ragathiel (Ragathiel): You were born into a family, nation, or other group that tried to impress evil ideals upon you, but you were inspired by Ragathiel to live a moral life despite their influence. You gain a +2 trait bonus on Sense Motive checks to see through an evil creature's Bluff attempts.

Ragathiel's Paladin Code

The paladins of Ragathiel are shining beacons of furious resolve on the battlefield, and they are careful stewards of valor everywhere. These paladins disproportionately come from cultures that are typically hostile to paladin training, including those of half-orcs, hobgoblins, Gebbites, and the Nidalese. The tenets of Ragathiel's paladins include the following affirmations.

- I will avenge evil wrought upon the innocent.
- I will not give my word lightly, but once it is given, I will uphold a promise until my last breath.
- Those proven guilty must be punished for their crimes. I will not turn a blind eye to wrongdoing.
- Rage is a virtue and a strength only when focused against the deserving. I will never seek disproportionate retribution.
- Redemption finds hearts from even the cruelest origins. I will strive not to act upon prejudice against fellow mortals based on race or origin.

SHIZURU

Shizuru, Empress of Heaven, is a prominent deity throughout the vast lands of Tian Xia and among Tien immigrants to other parts of Golarion. Her portfolio includes ancestors, honor, swordplay, and the sun. She also teaches the value of devoted love even beyond death and across great distances, as she has with the moon god Tsukiyo, her lover and the Prince of the Moon. Her worship is rare in the Inner Sea region, but many who venerate her there are paladins.

Ancestor's Blade (Shizuru): You were trained by your family with a weapon passed down from a venerable ancestor. You begin play with an heirloom masterwork weapon worth up to 400 gp. You gain a +1 trait bonus on attack rolls with weapons of this type (not just your initial heirloom weapon) when you smite evil.

Pristine Reputation (Shizuru): You come from an especially esteemed family, religious order, school, or other group that worships Shizuru, and draw upon that tradition to maintain your identity. The first time each day that you fail a saving throw against a charm or compulsion effect, you can reroll that saving throw. If you do so, you gain a +2 trait bonus on this roll and use this result as the actual result for that saving throw.

SHIZURU'S PALADIN CODE

The paladins of Shizuru are warriors who serve just lords, peacekeepers who oppose banditry, and those who advocate for honored ancestors. When great heroes fall, these dedicated paladins sometimes ritually preserve the bodies for later revivification. Their tenets include the following affirmations.

- My blade will be as steady as the sun and my training will be as consistent; I shall respect what I have mastered and seek to impart this training to others.
- I will honor my ancestors, who have come before me and provided for my life.
- The bonds of love extend across any distance, but I will not add to the burden by separating lovers.
- My personal honor reflects on my family and my liege; I will conscientiously maintain my reputation for the sake of theirs, even on the battlefield.
- As I respect the Empress of Heaven, so will I respect my sworn liege.

TRUDD

Trudd the Mighty is the youngest son of Torag and strongest of the dwarven deities. He is known for his oddly short beard; apocryphal stories claim he sold it to pay for an unknown boon. He protects Torag's hall in his father's absence and exemplifies bravery, defense, and strength.

Guardian Smite (Trudd): Paladins of Trudd taught you to be a blessed, living barrier against enemies who threaten those you hold dear. Once per day, when you strike a foe with smite evil, you can halve the total damage dealt to the foe to reduce that foe's speed to 5 feet for 1 round.

Mighty Protector (Trudd): When you were too young to fight, you witnessed a great tragedy befall an innocent and you swore to Trudd you'd become strong enough to prevent something like that from happening again. Once per day when you hit a foe with a melee attack, you can attempt an aid another action as a free action to increase an adjacent ally's AC against that foe. If you succeed, you grant the ally a +4 bonus to AC instead of a +2 bonus for that round.

TRUDD'S PALADIN CODE

The paladins of Trudd are stalwart protectors of the dwarven people and their greatest treasures. The tenets of Trudd's paladins include the following affirmations.

- My strength is my sacred offering. I will maintain my body as I would a sacred relic and use it only for admirable pursuits.
- To ensure the safety of those I protect, I will be among the first to charge and the last to retreat, save when such tactics would place those I protect at undue risk.
- I will hold any defensive line if it will save innocents or the homes of my people.
- Even the young can accomplish great things. I will never dismiss someone on account of youth.

VILDEIS

Vildeis, the Cardinal Martyr, is an angelic empyreal lord wholly devoted to the destruction of evil. She could not bear the sight of all the evils in the multiverse, and so she blinded herself.

Blind Zeal (Vildeis): You are blind but trained by followers of Vildeis to sense your surroundings by sound and touch. You need not attempt a skill check to move at full speed. You take a −4 penalty from blindness on only Acrobatics, Ride, Sleight of Hand, and Stealth checks. You gain Blind-Fight as a bonus feat. You lose the benefits of this trait whenever you can see, but regain them if you once again become blind.

Resilient Martyr (Vildeis): You interposed yourself between an innocent and a dangerous evil monster or force, lost a great deal of blood as a result, and barely survived. Now, your blood seems to replenish with blessed speed, a sure sign of Vildeis's favor. You recover twice as many hit points and points of ability damage as normal when you rest, or three times as many when you take total bed rest.

Vildeis's Paladin Code

The paladins of Vildeis are eager and self-denying martyrs in search of a good cause. Their tenets include the following affirmations.

- Sacrifice defies the selfishness of evil. I will not shy from a sacrifice that would help the greater good.
- Evil does not rest, so good cannot either. I will not be complacent, but rather seek out evil to oppose.
- Family is a rare refuge from the evils of the world, but it cannot keep me from my cause. I will not favor my own family over other innocents.

Yuelral

Yuelral the Wise is a major deity of the elves. She presides over all magic, especially that which draws upon the natural world, as well as natural wonders such as crystals. She also encourages skillful craft with wood, ivory, and leather. Paladins of Yuelral are not common, but those who serve her place are as devout as any.

Gemstone Collector (Yuelral): You have long found focus and inspiration in the natural beauty of rare gemstones. As long as you carry bejeweled objects worth a total combined value of 200 gp × your character level, you gain a +1 trait bonus on all Will saving throws and a +2 trait bonus on a single Charisma-based skill check of your choice.

Natural Magic (Yuelral): Yuelral's teachings revealed to you that all magic can ultimately be traced back to nature. Choose two 0-level druid spells. You treat each spell as being on your class spell list and as a spell known for all spellcasting classes you have.

Yuelral's Paladin Code

The paladins of Yuelral are protectors of elven magical knowledge and of natural and magical wonders such as the *aiudara*. Their tenets include the following affirmations.

- I will never defile the beauty of nature, nor cut a raw gemstone for aesthetic reasons.
- I will remain vigilant for talent in craft and magic. When I notice it, I will encourage its good use.
- I will respect the power of magic and never allow its misuse.
- I will preserve the wisdom of the elves for the greater good before all other treasures.

Oaths of Virtue

The following paladin codes can be chosen by paladins with the oathbound paladin archetype (*Pathfinder RPG Ultimate Magic* 60).

Oath against the Whispering Way

The Whispering Way is an enemy to all life in the world, and as a result many paladins feel called to contain its evil. This oath is identical to the oath against undeath (*Pathfinder RPG Ultimate Magic* 61) except as noted here.

Deities: Angradd, Arqueros, Iomedae, Sarenrae, Torag, Vildeis.

Aura against Necromancy (Su): At 8th level, the paladin gains a +4 morale bonus on saves against necromancy spells and spell-like abilities. Each ally within 10 feet of her gains a +2 morale bonus on these saves. This ability functions only while the paladin is conscious, not if she is unconscious or dead.

This ability replaces aura of resolve instead of aura of life.

Code of Conduct: Destroy agents of the Whispering Way and stop the spread of their philosophy.

Oath of the Mendevian Crusade

The Worldwound threatens all of Golarion with the uttermost depths of depravity, and so paladins across the world stand firm against it. This oath is identical to the oath against fiends (*Pathfinder RPG Ultimate Magic* 61) except as noted here.

Deities: Angradd, Arqueros, Iomedae, Kols, Ragathiel, Sarenrae, Torag, Vildeis.

Divine Bond (Su): At 5th level, the paladin adds *evil outsider bane* to the list of weapon special abilities that can be added to her weapon and removes *flaming* from the list.

This ability alters divine bond.

Mercy (Su): At 12th level, the paladin can choose the following mercy.

Possessed: If the subject is affected by *dominate person*, possessed, or otherwise magically controlled by an evil outsider, this mercy grants the victim a new saving throw against the effect to end the effect at once.

Code of Conduct: Oppose demonic influence in all its forms and seek a way to close the Worldwound.

Oath of the People's Council

The Eagle Knights and the people of Andoran hold their elected officials to extremely high standards of conduct. Paladins swearing the oath of the People's Council serve the common good by finding and thwarting those who abuse their authority. Many seek specifically to emulate Talmandor, the agathion patron of Andoran.

Deities: Abadar, Erastil, Iomedae, Ragathiel, Shelyn, Vildeis.

Skills: The oathbound paladin's class skills include Linguistics, Perception, and Perform, but not Handle Animal, Ride, or Spellcraft.

Stirring Monologue (Su): At 1st level, the paladin can deliver a stirring monologue on the ideals of justice and fairness, motivating allies and persuading others. This functions as bardic performance as per a bard of her paladin level using Perform (oratory). All the effects are language-dependent even if they would not normally be. The paladin gains the following performances at the indicated levels: inspire courage (1st), fascinate (4th), inspire competence (5th), suggestion (7th), dirge of dread (10th), inspire greatness (13th), frightening tune (16th), and mass suggestion (19th).

This ability replaces smite evil.

Aura of Truth (Su): At 11th level, the paladin automatically succeeds at saving throws to disbelieve illusions of the phantasm subschool and automatically gains a saving throw to disbelieve figment illusions when she observes them. Allies within 30 feet gain a +4 bonus on saving throws to disbelieve illusions of the phantasm subschool.

This ability replaces aura of justice.

Champion of Andoran (Su): At 20th level, an oathbound paladin becomes a champion of the people of Andoran. Her DR increases to 10/evil. Whenever she uses her stirring monologue, up to four creatures (including the paladin herself) affected by the monologue gain SR 30 against spells with the evil descriptor or spell-like abilities cast by evil outsiders or undead. Weapons wielded by those affected by her stirring monologue are treated as good, silver, and cold iron for the purpose of overcoming damage reduction. In addition, whenever the oathbound paladin channels positive energy or uses lay on hands to heal a creature, she heals it the maximum possible amount.

This ability alters holy champion.

Code of Conduct: Know the laws of Andoran and do not exempt authorities from the application of the law.

Oath Spells: 1st—*comprehend languages*; 2nd—*locate object*; 3rd—*tongues*; 4th—*true seeing*.

Oath of the Skyseeker

The dwarven people look to the legendary Sky Citadels as beacons of dwarven culture. Paladins with the oath of the skyseeker swear to defend those citadels their people retain and to help reclaim those the dwarves have lost, hoping to one day rebuild them on the greatest, most honorable ideals of the dwarven gods.

Deities: Angradd, Folgrit, Kols, Torag, Trudd.

Smite Evil Hordes (Su): When the paladin or an ally defeats the target of the paladin's smite evil ability, the paladin can change the target of her smite to a different target within 30 feet of the previously defeated target without using an action. The new target must be of the same creature type and subtype as the previous target. If no applicable target is within 30 feet, then the smite evil effect ends. The paladin's smite does not deal more damage to evil outsiders, dragons, or undead than to other evil creatures.

This ability alters smite evil.

Divine Bond (Su): At 5th level, the paladin adds *mighty cleaving* to the list of weapon special abilities that can be added to her weapon and removes *flaming* from the list.

This ability alters divine bond.

Mercy for the Lost (Sp): At 11th level, the paladin can use the Sky Citadels as a beacon leading her on the path to her deity. If she is on the Material Plane,

the paladin can use *find the path* once per day at her paladin level, but only to find her way to a known Sky Citadel. If she is not on the Material Plane, she can instead use this ability to use *plane shift* as per the spell to travel to a known Sky Citadel. If she is in a Sky Citadel, she can expend her daily use of this ability to use *plane shift* to travel to the realm of her deity.

This ability replaces aura of justice.

Stalwart (Ex): At 14th level, the paladin's quest has strengthened her body and mind. If she succeeds at a Fortitude or Will saving throw against an effect that has a reduced effect on a successful save, she instead avoids the effect entirely. A helpless paladin does not gain the benefit of the stalwart ability.

This ability replaces aura of faith.

Code of Conduct: Reclaim a Sky Citadel in the name of honorable dwarven ideals. Defend Sky Citadels already held by dwarves.

Oath Spells: 1st—*enlarge person*; 2nd—*find traps*; 3rd—*spiritual ally*[APG]; 4th—*blessing of fervor*[APG].

Acolytes of Apocrypha

Because most deities' influence extends across countless civilizations, gods rarely object when their worshipers innovate and adapt their spiritual beliefs to meet local needs. Such a cultural and religious evolution can spawn sects with bizarre religious interpretations that seem utterly alien to the faith's mainstream members.

Many of these beliefs can be found in specialized and usually quite rare religious texts known as apocryphas. The contents of these books often bring the teachings of the deity in question to bear on unexpected topics. In other cases, these addendums to holy texts are wholly logical extensions of a section of one faith's core tenets, but applied to another faith's teachings—perhaps even one diametrically opposed to the first faith. An apocryphal work is generally the same as a standard holy text in size and cost, but finding the exact one you might be seeking for a specific faith can be tricky indeed.

Apocryphal Subdomains

A divine spellcaster who studies an apocrypha, or who studies under a scholar well versed in such a text, can gain access to unusual subdomains associated with a deity. Whether or not the mainstream church accepts any one apocryphal text as canonical or not can vary, even within the same religion; for some believers, though, these words are as true as anything about their belief.

A domain-using PC can gain access to one of these subdomains via the following faith trait. An NPC does not need such a trait, provided that the NPC has a flavorful background that explains how he or she came in contact with the apocryphal information. Subdomains were introduced on page 86 of the *Pathfinder RPG Advanced Player's Guide*.

Acolyte of Apocrypha (Faith): Your religious studies hinged on teachings rarely recognized by your faith. You can select one of the apocryphal subdomains detailed below, provided the subdomain is associated with your patron deity. In some cases, you can select a subdomain associated with a deity despite that deity not offering the associated domain—these exceptions are noted with an asterisk (*), and you gain domain powers and domain spells from the associated domain as usual, even though your deity normally doesn't grant access to that domain. When selecting a subdomain associated with two domains, a priest can choose only a subdomain that modifies a domain to which he has access. All deities referenced in the following subdomains appear in *Pathfinder Campaign Setting: Inner Sea Gods* or *Pathfinder Campaign Setting: Dragon Empires Gazetteer*.

Alchemy Subdomain

Example Apocrypha (Qi Zhong): Just as the samsarans of Zi Ha know that they will be reborn to perform more good deeds, so too can their alchemists store divine power through the transmutation and rebirth of mundane elements in simple tonics. More than a millennium ago, a sect of Qi Zhong's faithful began combining their god's healing magic with the enduring science of alchemy. In the intervening years, they have codified their composite art in the five scrolls known as The Five-Spoked Cycle, now in its 22nd official revision.

Associated Domains: Artifice, Magic.

Associated Deities: Brigh, Haagenti, Norgorber* (Artifice only), Orgesh* (Magic only), Qi Zhong.

Replacement Power: The following granted power replaces the artificer's touch power of the Artifice domain or the hand of the acolyte power of the Magic domain.

Divine Alchemy (Su): You can perform a 1-minute ritual that infuses a flask of water with one of your prepared spells, creating an improvised potion that lasts until consumed or the next time you prepare spells. You can use this ability only with spells that target one or more creatures, and the maximum spell level you can infuse in this way is equal to 1 + 1 for every 4 cleric levels you have. These potions are treated as alchemist extracts for the purpose of your domain spells. You can use this ability a number of times per day equal to 3 + your Wisdom modifier.

Replacement Domain Spells: 2nd—*touch injection*[UC], 4th—*amplify elixir*[APG], 6th—*delayed consumption*[APG].

Captivation Subdomain

Example Apocrypha (Norgorber): Norgorber's faithful take considerable risks just to maintain their secrets, so the flashy antics of those who have read *The Dark Lure* seem appalling to most. These reckless devotees ostensibly revere the Reaper of Reputation, yet they insist that the best way to hide in plain sight is by being the center of attention and sharing so much harmless information that none think to look any deeper. As a result, the cult attracts Norgorber's rare thrill-seekers and dare-takers. His other worshipers suffer these brazen actions, knowing that their brethren would make ideal scapegoats should the congregations of more legitimate churches be discovered.

Associated Domain: Charm.

Associated Deities: Calistria, Kofusachi, Nalinivati, Norgorber, Shelyn.

Replacement Power: The following granted power replaces the charming smile power of the Charm domain.

Entrancing Aura (Su): At 8th level, you can emit an imperceptible 30-foot aura of distraction as a standard action for a number of rounds equal to your cleric level. These rounds need not be consecutive. Enemies within this aura take a –5 penalty on Perception checks and are treated as though they had 2 fewer Hit Dice (minimum 1 Hit Die) for the purpose of your effects that would give them the fascinated condition. At 16th level, they are instead treated as if they had 3 fewer Hit Dice for such effects.

Replacement Domain Spells: 1st—*hypnotism*, 2nd—*hypnotic pattern*, 4th—*rainbow pattern*.

Hubris Subdomain

Example Apocrypha (Iomedae): As the Second Mendevian Crusade drew to a close, the crusaders found they had exhausted many of their strongest warriors, forcing them to recruit mercenaries of less noble intentions. At the same time, demons began infiltrating Mendev's ranks, spreading lies, and seeding betrayal. The Third Crusade collapsed nearly as soon as it began, crippled by witch-hunts and bloodthirsty inquisitions. The Church of Iomedae has since reprimanded the overzealous interrogators who led those pogroms, yet a small cult of apostates refuses to accept forgiveness for the faith's lapse. Calling themselves the Children of the Third Crusade, these curious acolytes self-flagellate to seek humility, yet they then lord their righteousness over their peers in shows of disquieting vanity. The crusaders suffer these fanatics' presence, acknowledging them as a living lesson of the crusade's past failures.

Associated Domains: Glory, Nobility.

Associated Deities: Dispater, General Susumu, Iomedae, Jaidz, Lissala, Olheon, Ydersius.

Replacement Power: You gain Intimidate as a class skill; this replaces the Glory domain's increased save DC to resist channel positive energy. The following granted power replaces the divine presence power of the Glory domain or the leadership power of the Nobility domain.

Divine Demand (Su): At 6th level, you can petition your divine patron for far greater power than you deserve. Activating this ability is a swift action that you must use as you cast a spell that has a reduced (but not negated) effect on a successful save. The saving throw DC of the spell increases by 2, and you gain a +2 bonus on caster level checks to overcome spell resistance with the spell. Any creature that succeeds at the saving throw instead avoids the effect entirely. If half or more of the targets are unaffected, you become shaken for a number of rounds equal to the spell's level. If all of the targets are unaffected, you instead lose the ability to cast divine spells, channel energy, and use domain powers for 1d4+1 rounds; you can end this loss as a full-round action by loudly apologizing to your patron deity as a full-round action that provokes attacks of opportunity. You can use this ability once per day at 6th level, and one additional time per day for every 4 levels beyond 6th.

Replacement Domain Spells: 4th—*hollow heroism*[UI], 7th—*greater hollow heroism*[UI], 9th—*overwhelming presence*[UM]. If you are evil, replace the domain spells *bless weapon* and *holy aura* with *aid* and *unholy aura* respectively.

Insect Subdomain

Example Apocrypha (Ghlaunder): While Ghlaunder's faithful honor the pests that carry contagion, a cult deep within the Mwangi Expanse has dedicated itself to raising giant mosquitoes. Each cultist adopts such a beast and allows it to feed on a portion of his blood every day while he seeks out and exposes himself to ever-deadlier contagions. Few survive this excruciating regimen of self-sacrifice, dictated by their unholy text *The Sipping Sacrifice*. Those who can sustain it hope that as their bonded companions ingest and gestate countless plagues, the vermin might metamorphose into Ghlaunder's most beloved minions: blightspawn (*Pathfinder RPG Bestiary 5* 43).

Associated Domain: Animal.

Associated Deities: Achaekek*, Aldinach, Deskari*, Ghlaunder, Kitumu, Mazmezz.

Replacement Power: The domain spells provided by the Insect domain affect vermin rather than animals, treating them as if they were not immune to spells with the mind-affecting descriptor. Any such spell that allows a Will save can instead be negated by the target vermin with a successful Fortitude save at the same DC. The following granted power replaces the speak with animals power of the Animal domain.

Exoskeleton (Su): As a swift action, you can grow an exoskeleton that grants you a +1 enhancement bonus to your natural armor and 1d4 temporary hit points + 1 for every 2 cleric levels you have. The natural armor bonus increases by 1 for every 5 cleric levels you have. The exoskeleton retracts after 1 round, ending its benefits. You can use this ability a number of times per day equal to 3 + your Wisdom modifier.

Replacement Domain Spells: 4th—*giant vermin*, 5th—*vermin shape II*[UM], 8th—*summon nature's ally VIII* (1d3 goliath stag beetles; *Pathfinder RPG Bestiary 2* 44).

Legend Subdomain

Example Apocrypha (Gorum): To Gorumites, even the greatest glory is fleeting; one must continually prove oneself in battle, and a warrior's fame quickly fades after her death. In the Lands of the Linnorm Kings, a controversial sect of priests have sequestered themselves from the raiding culture to chronicle the deeds of great warriors and transform these tales into a living holy text known as *The Myth in Iron*. Contrary to their blood-spattered colleagues' claims that such chronicles would breed complacency, these priests believe that such legends will inspire young raiders to match and exceed the deeds of their predecessors while honoring the fallen.

Associated Domain: Glory.

Associated Deities: General Susumu, Gorum, Shizuru.

Replacement Power: In campaigns that use the optional hero point system (*Pathfinder RPG Advanced Player's Guide* 322), you gain Hero's Fortune (*Advanced Player's Guide* 324) as a bonus feat. Otherwise, you gain Marked for Glory (*Pathfinder RPG Mythic Adventures* 69) as a bonus feat, even if you do not meet its prerequisites. These replace the Glory domain's increased save DC when channeling positive energy. In addition, the following granted power replaces the divine presence power of the Glory domain.

Witness the Legend (Su): At 8th level, as a move action, you can extol the virtues of yourself or an ally within 60 feet that you can see. This causes the target to shed light like a torch for 1 minute, and while the effect lasts, you can expend a daily use of your touch of glory domain ability as an immediate action to add 1d6 to an attack, saving throw, skill check, or ability check attempted by the target; for a roll to confirm a critical hit or save against a fear effect, you instead add 1d12. You can use this ability once per day at 8th level and one additional time per day for every 4 levels beyond 8th.

Replacement Domain Spells: 2nd—*aid*, 3rd—*contagious zeal*[OA], 4th—*righteous vigor*[APG], 6th—*unshakable zeal*[OA]. If you are evil, replace the domain spells *holy smite, holy sword,* and *holy aura* with *unholy blight, unholy sword*[UM], and *unholy aura* respectively.

Lightning Subdomain

Example Apocrypha (Hei Feng): The tengu of Kwanlai suffered for centuries under the yoke of Lung Wa's rule, and it was only the Feather and Starlight Rebellion that finally freed the region. Among the Hei Fengan priests who joined the uprising were numerous members of the

Sunderstorm Covenant, who believed lightning was the purest of their god's weapons that must be wielded in defense of the homeland—even if doing so would destroy the wielder as well. The popularity of this group has sharply declined over the past decade, for its members zealously encourage violent responses to even the mildest perceived slights, at the cost of Kwanlai's tenuous stability.

Associated Domain: Air.

Associated Deities: Gozreh, Hei Feng, Rovagug, Rull.

Replacement Power: The following granted power replaces the electricity resistance power of the Air domain.

Lightning Rod (Su): As a swift action when you cast a spell with the electricity descriptor, you can designate one creature within line of sight. The spell's damage against that creature increases by 50%, as if affected by the Empower Spell feat. This additional damage results from divine power that is not subject to being reduced by electricity resistance, and you take an equal amount of electricity damage immediately after you cast the spell. The spell can deal this additional damage only once, even if it could affect the target multiple times. You can use this ability once per day at 8th level and one additional time per day for every 4 cleric levels you have beyond 8th.

Replacement Domain Spells: 1st—*shocking grasp*, 2nd—*flame blade* (deals electricity damage and gains the electricity descriptor instead of fire), 3rd—*lightning bolt*.

Medicine Subdomain

Example Apocrypha (Immonhiel): Following an internecine bout of sectarian violence thousands of years ago, Rahadoum banned all religious expression in its borders, including divine spellcasting. Most who defy this law do so in secret, including a small cult of Immonhiel's priests who recently infiltrated Azir's poorest districts. Referring to themselves as the Silent Surgeons, these faithful willingly eschew holy symbols, spellcasting, and proselytization, yet dedicate themselves to nonmagically healing any who ask. These disciples believe that through selfless dedication to others and personal hardship they can heal Rahadoum's emotional scars and convince the country to acknowledge the gods once more.

Associated Domain: Healing.

Associated Deities: Dalenydra, Immonhiel, Irori, Korada, Qi Zhong, Sarenrae.

Replacement Power: The following granted power replaces the rebuke death power of the Healing domain.

Blessed Surgery (Su): Your divine patron guides your healing hands, allowing you to perform minor miracles with mundane cures. You can use this ability as a free action when using the Heal skill in order to roll the check twice and take the higher result. When you're using this ability, any use of the Heal skill requiring 1 hour instead takes at most 1 minute. You can use this ability a number of times per day equal to 3 + your Wisdom modifier.

Replacement Domain Spells: 1st—*diagnose disease*UM, 2nd—*placebo effect*OA.

Monsoon Subdomain

Example Apocrypha (Rull): The Hold of Belkzen echoes with battle for much of the year, but when the seasonal rains return, the orc tribes all honor the Flood Truce, hunting and trading in peace until the land dries. While most priests of Rull revel in his destructive lightning, a growing contingent of "flood prophets" envision him as an orc god of renewal. After all, his clouds shelter sensitive eyes from the sun, and his storms bring life-giving water that lures in prey and washes away filth from encampments. For the few months the rains last, most orcs respect the flood prophets' bizarre ceremonies. When war returns once more, these apostates shelter in the mountains and wait for signs that the healing storms will return.

Associated Domain: Weather

Associated Deities: Daikitsu, Gozreh, Hei Feng, Rull.

Replacement Power: The following granted power replaces the lightning lord ability of the Weather domain.

Refreshing Rain (Su): At 8th level, as standard action, you can call a brief shower of rain in a 30-foot radius. Creatures in the area are healed of an amount of nonlethal damage equal to double your cleric level and are no longer exhausted, fatigued, nauseated, or sickened. You can use this ability once per day at 8th level, and one additional time per day for every 4 levels beyond 8th.

Replacement Domain Spells: 3rd—*hydraulic torrent*APG, 4th—*control water*, 5th—*fickle winds*APG, 9th—*tsunami*APG.

Petrification Subdomain

Example Apocrypha (Soralyon): Magnimar is famous for its monuments, many of which impart blessings upon the city's citizens. A faction of Soralyon's worshipers engage in (or have already undergone esoteric rituals to transform themselves and any who request the honor into new monuments. Several copies of their recently recorded philosophies entitled *We Stand Unblinking* have begun circulating the city. The modest folio suggests that some catastrophe in the distant future will threaten all of Golarion, at which point Soralyon's true faithful will awaken from stone to protect Golarion with their lives.

Associated Domain: Earth.

Associated Deities: Ayrzul, Minderhal, Soralyon, Xoveron.

Replacement Power: The following granted power replaces the acid dart power of the Earth domain.

Fossil Form (Su): At the beginning of your turn as a swift action, you can infuse your flesh with minerals, granting you cumbersome security. Until the beginning of your next turn, you are staggered, gain hardness 2, and gain a +2 bonus on saving throws against petrification. This hardness increases by 2 and your saving throw bonus increases by 1 for every 4 cleric levels you have. You can use this ability a number of times per day equal to 3 + your Wisdom modifier.

Replacement Domain Spells: 4th—*calcific touch*APG, 5th—*stoneskin*, 6th—*flesh to stone*, 8th—*statue*.

Portal Subdomain

Example Apocrypha (Abadar): Separated by war, boundaries, and untamed frontier, Golarion's greatest cities enjoy only a fraction of the prosperity they might if united. The Apostles of Axis have spent several decades lobbying and constructing permanent gateways between the planet's metropolises. Very few of their urban benefactors appreciate this "service," seeing the backdoors both as security threats and as innovations that threaten to undermine the local transportation industries. Absalom, Oppara, Sothis, and others have tried to destroy these borderline-heretical Abadarans' gateways, even going so far as to hire adventurers to sniff out the latest portal.

Associated Domain: Travel.

Associated Deities: Abadar, Alseta*, Barbatos, Yog-Sothoth.

Replacement Power: The following granted powers replace the base speed increase and agile feet power of the Travel domain.

Sacred Threshold (Su): As a standard action, you can bless a door, a window, or another portal with a touch. For 1 minute, you can increase or decrease the DC of any check to unlock or force open the portal by an amount equal to half your cleric level. In addition, your first ally to pass through the portal during this time gains an amount of temporary hit points equal to 1d4 + 1 for every 2 cleric levels you have. These temporary hit points last for 1 minute. You can use this ability a number of times per day equal to 3 + your Wisdom modifier.

Travel as One (Su): When you cast a spell with the teleportation descriptor, treat your caster level as 3 higher for the purpose of determining how many additional creatures you can bring with you. In addition, you and any creatures you teleport gain a number of temporary hit points equal to your level that disappear after you reach your destination; these offset any damage you might take from teleportation mishaps or attempting to teleport into a solid body.

Replacement Domain Spells: 1st—*open and shut*UI, 2nd—*knock*, 3rd—*urban step*UI, 9th—*teleportation circle*.

RITES SUBDOMAIN

Example Apocrypha (Nethys): Magic is sacred to all Nethysians, yet to the Gebbite arcane philosopher Oushal, magic's greatest quality—arguably its only redeeming quality—was its capacity to outlast all else; she believed that which was ephemeral was meaningless, whereas that which was everlasting would grant its creator glory. During the Age of Destiny, she squandered her family's fortune creating 10 everlasting enchantments of impossible intricacy. Fearing jealous rivals would steal her secrets, she embraced lichdom centuries before Geb and Nex ever fought. When her homeland began to revere undeath millennia later, scholars unearthed Oushal's maddeningly baroque treatise, the *Libram of Ten Eternities*, and acknowledged it as an innovative endorsement of eternal unlife. The demilich Oushal now resides in Mechitar, accepts donations to maintain her eternal spells, and occasionally shares her wisdom with pilgrims.

Associated Domain: Magic.

Associated Deities: Abraxas, Asmodeus, Nalinivati, Nethys, Nyarlathotep, Sivanah.

Replacement Power: When casting a Rites domain spell with a costly material component—or casting *permanency* on any domain spell—reduce the cost of the necessary components by 20%. The following granted power replaces the hand of the acolyte power of the Magic domain.

Enduring Ritual (Su): As a swift action when you cast a spell with a duration of at least 1 minute per caster level, you can increase the spell's effective caster level by 1 for the purpose of determining its duration and preventing attempts to dispel it. The effective caster level increases by an additional 1 for every 10 cleric levels you have (maximum +3). You can use this ability a number of times per day equal to 3 + your Wisdom modifier.

Replacement Domain Spells: 1st—*sanctify corpse*^{UM}, 5th—*permanency*, 8th—*binding*.

SELF-REALIZATION SUBDOMAIN

Example Apocrypha (Falayna): "Loss begets growth," say Lastwall's Steel Widows, an order of warriors dedicated to the empyreal lord Falayna. The Steel Widows believe that experiencing loss is key to becoming a true warrior. They operate a small orphanage in Vigil, teaching children that tragedy may have shaped their pasts, but it need never dictate their futures. The organization welcomes faithful of any gender, though its ranks are predominantly female.

Associated Domains: Liberation, Strength.

Associated Deities: Arshea, Falayna, Haagenti, Irori, Kurgess, Shei, Urgathoa.

Replacement Power: The following granted power replaces the liberation power of the Liberation domain or the strength surge ability of the Strength domain.

Perfected Form (Su): You maintain an unshakable sense of who you are, and no force can compel you to be anything else. You gain a +1 sacred (if your patron is good or neutral) or profane (if your patron is evil) bonus on saving throws against polymorph, petrification, and transmutation effects. This bonus increases by 1 for every 5 cleric levels you have (maximum +5). Once per day when you succeed at a saving throw against such an effect, you can gain a surge of self-confidence as an immediate action that grants you a number of temporary hit points equal to your cleric level and a +2 morale bonus on attack rolls, skill checks, and saving throws; both effects last for 1 minute.

Replacement Domain Spells: 4th—*paragon surge* (*Pathfinder RPG Advanced Race Guide* 48; always matches your actual race), 6th—*primal scream*^{UM}, 7th—*transformation*.

THIRST SUBDOMAIN

Example Apocrypha (Lalaci): Lalaci provides rest and shade to the weary, yet the same oases and refuges his faithful favor often attract profiteering mortals and predatory fiends that prey upon the tired. As the Water Lords of Thuvia have become increasingly cutthroat, Lalaci has attracted dozens of inquisitors who patrol these restful sanctuaries and inflict the same parched deaths upon those who would deny hospitality to others. This retributive policy, recorded in the work *For All to Drink*, appeals to some members of Sarenrae's Cult of the Dawnflower, but thus far this interpretation of their goddess's wrath has not spread far.

Associated Subdomain: Sun.

Associated Deities: Aldinach, Lalaci, Nurgal, Sarenrae.

Replacement Power: The following granted power replaces the sun's blessing power and alters the nimbus of light power of the Sun domain.

Wilting Glare (Su): As a standard action, you can leach moisture and vitality from a living, corporeal creature you can see within 30 feet. The target takes an amount of nonlethal damage equal to 1d6 + 1 for every 2 cleric levels you have and becomes fatigued until the beginning of your next turn (Fortitude negates). Plant creatures and those with the aquatic or water subtype take lethal damage from this ability, and they are fatigued for a number of rounds equal to your Wisdom modifier. You can use this ability a number of times per day equal to 3 + your Wisdom modifier.

Withering Nimbus (Su): This ability functions as the nimbus of light domain ability, but it damages plants and creatures with the aquatic or water subtype, not undead.

Replacement Domain Spells: 3rd—*cup of dust*^{APG}, 9th—*horrid wilting*.

THORNS SUBDOMAIN

Example Apocrypha (Zyphus): Whereas many Zyphens tailor their dreadful accidents to each victim, a sect of the Grim Harvestman's faithful teach that they must encourage nature itself to indiscriminately inflict accidental pain and death upon the unwary. The bloodstained journal of a now-forgotten Zyphen, entitled *Sowing Despair*, relates the writer's decades of breeding and planting vicious nettles all around the Lake

Encarthan region. The work has since been recopied and distributed widely—especially in the River Kingdoms, where Zyphens delight in watching pioneers die horribly in the unforgiving frontier.

Associated Domain: Plant.

Associated Deities: The Green Mother, Shub-Niggurath, Zyphus.

Replacement Power: The following granted power replaces the wooden fist power of the Plant domain.

Cruel Thicket (Su): As a standard action, you can cause the ground in a 5-foot-radius burst centered on you to sprout twisting, thorny vines. Any creature moving through it must travel at half speed or take bleed damage equal to half your cleric level; if you activate this ability in an area with numerous plants (grass, weeds, trees, etc.), the area also becomes difficult terrain. These effects last for 1 minute, after which the vines crumble to dust. Creatures able to move through natural undergrowth unhindered ignore the effects of this ability. You can use this ability a number of times per day equal to 3 + your Wisdom modifier.

Replacement Domain Spells: 1st—*thorn javelin*^{ACG}, 3rd—*thorny entanglement*^{ACG}, 4th—*thorn body*^{APG}.

Truth Subdomain

Example Apocrypha (Sivanah): Many of Sivanah's faithful teach that there is no ultimate truth, only further illusions to be unveiled. Those fanatics known as the Seekers of the Seventh Veil insist that this conventional wisdom is only another deception and that Sivanah herself hides absolute knowledge behind her innermost veil. The largest concentration of apostates has congregated in Kaer Maga over the last three years, where their intermittently lucid ramblings have unsettled even the unshakable locals. Their displays have begun interfering with the troll augurs' business, and it is only a matter of time before these violent prophets retaliate.

Associated Subdomain: Madness.

Associated Deities: Groetus, Lamashtu, Sifkesh, Sivanah.

Replacement Power: The following granted power replaces the aura of madness power of the Madness domain.

Dawning Realization (Su): At 8th level, you can impart a shared vision of unfathomable ineffability to a living creature you touch as a standard action, after which your turn immediately ends. You are dazed and the target confused for 1 round by what you both learn. On the following round, you are both staggered for 1 round by the ramifications of your discovery. On the

third round, you are confused and the target dazed for 1 round as you attempt to regain your bearings. Each round, the target can attempt a Will save with a DC equal to 10 + 1/2 your cleric level + your Wisdom modifier to negate that round's effects for both of you, though the effect does not end until the end of the third round. This is a mind-affecting effect that you can use a number of times per day equal to 1/2 your class level.

Replacement Domain Spells: 3rd—*wall of nausea*^{ACG}, 5th—*contact other plane*, 6th—*litany of madness*^{UC}.

Divine Fighting Manuals

Many of Golarion's religions have associated fighting traditions, born from the reverence that each congregation has for its deity's favored weapon. Traditionally, a clergy's fighting style is recorded in a special text known as a divine fighting manual, which includes parables and teachings of its deity alongside numerous martial secrets.

Emulating the Gods

Anyone faithful to a deity can learn that god's divine fighting style by taking the Divine Fighting Technique feat (see below). Alternatively, a cleric, inquisitor, or warpriest who worships a deity can choose to give up either the first power of one of her domains or a minor blessing benefit to gain access to her god's divine fighting technique without having to meet the technique's prerequisites (including the Divine Fighting Technique feat). In addition, a warpriest can give up a major blessing to gain the advanced benefit without meeting its prerequisites. In some cases, other classes can gain the benefits by sacrificing class features, as noted in the Optional Prerequisite or Optional Advanced Prerequisite section of the appropriate divine fighting technique.

Divine Fighting Technique (Combat)

You have trained in the divine fighting technique of a specific deity.

Prerequisite: Must worship a single patron deity that has an established divine fighting technique.

Benefit: You can use your patron deity's fighting technique and receive any benefit associated with that technique for which you qualify, as described in the Divine Fighting Techniques section below.

Divine Fighting Techniques

The following divine fighting techniques (in addition to those described on page 10 of *Pathfinder Player Companion: Weapon Master's Handbook*) are available to all characters with the Divine Fighting Technique feat or who meet the optional prerequisites.

Asmodeus's Mandate

Although soldiers and mercenaries alike in Cheliax claim that the martial techniques detailed within *Wrath and Punishment*, the most well-known fighting manual of the Church of Asmodeus, are as old as time itself, martial experts across the Inner Sea region note that *Wrath and Punishment* is less than 3 decades old. Of course, few in Cheliax dare to publicly make such claims. Outside of Cheliax, copies of *Wrath and Punishment* tend to be found in Hellknight enclaves.

Initial Benefit: Whenever you threaten a critical hit with a light mace or heavy mace on a foe, that foe becomes sickened for 1 round. If you confirm the critical hit, the sickened effect lasts for 2 rounds. The duration of the sickened effect doesn't stack with multiple critical threats.

Advanced Prerequisites: Int 13; Combat Expertise; Divine Fighting Technique; Improved Feint; base attack bonus +10 or Bluff 10 ranks.

Advanced Benefit: An opponent that you hit with a light mace or heavy mace who is denied his Dexterity bonus to AC is also hindered by the attack. You can attempt a dirty trick[APG] combat maneuver check as a swift action that doesn't provoke an attack of opportunity immediately after damage from the attack is resolved.

Desna's Shooting Star

Among the divine fighting manuals of the Inner Sea, few are as ancient as *Clamor of the Spheres*, a collection of fighting techniques favored by Desna's faithful. True to its name, the manual focuses on interpreting the chaos and sounds of combat, but nevertheless provides insightful and downright brilliant methods of defense with Desna's favored weapon, using techniques that treat a fight with a starknife more as a beautiful dance than a battle.

Optional Prerequisite: A chaotic good bard of at least 2nd level who worships Desna can replace a versatile performance with the following initial benefit.

Initial Benefit: You can add your Charisma bonus to attack rolls and damage rolls when wielding a starknife. If you do so, you don't modify attack rolls and damage rolls with your starknife with your Strength modifier, your Dexterity modifier (if you have Weapon Finesse), or any other ability score (if you have an ability that allows you to modify attack rolls and damage rolls with that ability score).

Advanced Prerequisites: Dex 17; Divine Fighting Technique; Point-Blank Shot; Rapid Shot; base attack bonus +11 or Sleight of Hand 11 ranks.

Optional Advanced Prerequisite: A chaotic good bard of at least 10th level who worships Desna can replace a versatile performance with the following advanced benefit without meeting its prerequisites.

Advanced Benefit: You can impart a powerful spin to a thrown starknife so that multiple blades strike the target rather than just a single blade of the four, dealing extra damage with the other blades. As a full-round action, you can make a single attack with a thrown starknife, rolling 1d4 to determine how many effective strikes you gain with the attack (if you roll a 1, then only one blade strikes). If the attack hits, all of the effective strikes damage the target. Apply precision-based damage (such as sneak attack damage) and critical hit damage only once for this attack. The damage bonus from your appropriate ability score modifier applies to each strike, as do other damage bonuses, such as a bard's inspire competence bonus. Damage reduction and resistances apply separately to each strike.

Erastil's Distracting Shot

Sometimes used as a companion piece to the *Parables of Erastil*, the lesser-known *Horns of the Elk* is a manual completely dedicated to archery. Lacking the folktales that the *Parables* are celebrated for, the *Horns of the Elk* instead focuses on covering a wide array of beginner and advanced archery tactics. A copy of the manual can be found virtually anywhere a shrine to Erastil exists.

Optional Prerequisite: A lawful good ranger who worships Erastil can choose Divine Fighting Technique as the bonus feat granted by his combat style if he chooses archery as his combat style.

Initial Benefit: As a standard action, you can fire a distracting shot from your longbow or shortbow; when you do, select one ally who is adjacent to the creature you are targeting with the distracting shot. If you hit the creature, the chosen ally gains a +2 bonus to her Armor Class against that creature. This bonus to her Armor Class lasts until the start of your next turn.

Advanced Prerequisites: Dex 17, Divine Fighting Technique, Point-Blank Shot, Precise Shot, base attack bonus +10.

Optional Advanced Prerequisite: A lawful good ranger who worships Erastil and has the Divine Fighting Technique feat can replace the bonus feat granted by his combat style at 10th level with the following advanced benefit without meeting its prerequisites.

Advanced Benefit: When you fire a distracting shot at a creature and hit the creature, you grant a +4 Armor Class bonus to the selected adjacent ally and a +2 Armor Class bonus to all other allies within 30 feet of the selected adjacent ally against attacks by the targeted creature.

Irori's Perfected Fist

Practically synonymous with Irori and his faith, *The Woven Fist* is among the best known of all diving fighting manuals. Many learned monks were taught their first martial techniques using drills and regiments from this manual, which some claim was written by Irori's own hand before his ascension to divinity. Although most commonly found in temples to Irori and secluded monasteries, copies of *The Woven Fist* often make their way into less scrupulous hands because of their effectiveness.

Optional Prerequisite: A lawful neutral brawler or monk can replace a bonus feat with the following initial benefit.

Initial Benefit: You can take a –2 penalty on all attack rolls made with your unarmed strikes in order to deal the average amount of damage with each successful attack instead of rolling your weapon damage. For instance, if your unarmed strike would normally deal 1d4 points of weapon damage, you instead deal 2 points of weapon damage. Apply bonuses and modifiers to this result as if you had rolled your damage normally. You must choose to use this benefit before making an attack roll, and its effects last until your next turn. You do not average additional damage dice (such as those granted by a sneak attack) when using this ability.

Advanced Prerequisites: Critical Focus; Divine Fighting Technique; Weapon Focus (unarmed strike); base attack bonus +10 or monk level 10th.

Advanced Optional Prerequisite: A lawful neutral brawler or monk of at least 10th level who worships Irori and has the Divine Fighting Technique feat can replace a bonus feat with the following advanced benefit without meeting its prerequisites.

Advanced Benefit: You no longer take a –2 penalty on attack rolls with your unarmed strikes when you choose to deal the average amount of damage. If you critically hit a creature when using this ability, you automatically inflict maximum weapon damage for that critical hit (although you must still roll sneak attack dice or any other dice-based additional damage).

Lamashtu's Carving

One of the grisliest divine fighting manuals is *Fecundity of Corpses*, a harrowing tome that depicts the fighting styles favored by the followers of Lamashtu, the Mother of Monsters. In addition to detailing many of the more gruesome rites favored by the Demon Queen, *Fecundity of Corpses* includes hundreds of techniques recorded in blood by cultists of Lamashtu from across the Inner Sea region. Though no standardized edition of this manual exists because of the cult's discordant hierarchy, each tome manages to perfectly capture similar techniques for sowing fear and blood in Lamashtu's name.

Initial Benefit: As a standard action, you can make a single attack with a falchion or a kukri in order to deal bleed damage to the target. When you make this attack, you do not apply your ability modifier (normally Strength, but potentially other modifiers) to the hit point damage dealt by your attack—instead, add an amount of bleed damage equal to this modifier. The bleeding can be stopped by a successful DC 15 Heal check or any amount of magical healing. Bleed damage from this benefit doesn't stack with itself.

Advanced Prerequisites: Str 13, Dazing Assault[APG], Divine Fighting Technique, Power Attack.

Advanced Benefit: Whenever you hit a bleeding creature with a melee attack using a falchion or a kukri, that creature must succeed at a Fortitude save (DC = 10 +

your base attack bonus) or become staggered for 1 round. Multiple attacks do not cause this condition to stack, and a creature that successfully saves against this staggering effect is immune to this effect for 1 round.

Norgorber's Silent Shiv

Entombed within a volume known as *The Reaper's Hand*, the divine fighting techniques of Norgorber are among the most elusive in the Inner Sea region, but are theorized to cover the techniques that acolytes of Father Skinsaw use to move and strike unseen. Copies of this manual are rare, and those who spill its secrets to anyone unworthy often meet a swift and bloody end at the hands of the faith's inquisitors.

Optional Prerequisite: A neutral evil rogue of at least 2nd level who worships Norgorber can replace a rogue talent with the following initial benefit.

Initial Benefit: Whenever you attack an opponent that is completely unaware of your presence (such as when you are using the Stealth skill or invisible), your attack deals damage as if you were one size category larger. This benefit applies only to the first attack that you make against the target, and only with attacks made with light or one-handed weapons intended for creatures of your size (including thrown attacks).

Advanced Prerequisites: Divine Fighting Technique, Stealth 10 ranks.

Optional Advanced Prerequisite: A neutral evil rogue of at least 10th level who worships Norgorber can replace an advanced rogue talent with the following advanced benefit without meeting its prerequisites.

Advanced Benefit: At the start of each round, choose one opponent that you can see and attempt a Stealth check as a swift action. If the result of your check exceeds the target's CMD, treat the target as if it were completely unaware of your presence for the purpose of the initial benefit of this divine fighting technique. If you beat the target's CMD by 5 or more, you also treat it as being completely unaware of your presence for the purposes of all class features and feats you have.

Rovagug's Thunder

Most copies of *Ravage and Ruin*, the divine fighting manual of the Rough Beast Rovagug, are scrawled in blood upon flensed skins by orc priests—and indeed the vile techniques described within originated from the Hold of Belkzen not long after the orcs first seized that land as their own. Reviled across the Inner Sea, *Ravage and Ruin* sees additional use among savage Ulfen clans who have fallen to the Rough Beast's urges to become corrupt, lunatic cannibals who relish despoiling beauty in Rovagug's name.

Initial Benefit: Whenever you succeed at a dirty trick^{APG} combat maneuver check against an opponent, you deal an amount of nonlethal damage equal to 1d6 + your Charisma modifier. In addition, whenever your dirty

trick combat maneuver check beats an opponent's CMD by 5 or more, you can forgo increasing the duration of your condition by 1 or more rounds to instead impose a –2 penalty on all of that opponent's Charisma-based checks. This penalty doesn't stack with itself, and it lasts for a number of minutes equal to your Charisma modifier (minimum of 1 minute) or until the target receives any form of magical healing.

Advanced Prerequisites: Power Attack, Divine Fighting Technique, base attack bonus +10.

Optional Advanced Prerequisites: A chaotic evil barbarian of at least 10th level who worships Rovagug can replace a rage power with the following advanced benefit without meeting its prerequisites.

Advanced Benefit: Anytime you use Power Attack with a great axe or a natural attack, you ignore an amount of the target's hardness or damage reduction equal to the penalty Power Attack imparts to your attack roll. This benefit stacks with Penetrating Strike and Greater Penetrating Strike.

Sarenrae's Mercy

Although the Dawnflower is the goddess of healing and redemption, she is not a goddess of peace, and her followers are taught that combat may be the only way to ensure the safety of those who look to the faith for protection. In such situations, the faithful of Sarenrae are expected to end combat swiftly and efficiently, to avoid drawing out the pain and agony of battle. When one can end a battle without resorting to killing, the opportunity for redemption of the defeated foe still remains. The pages of *Dawnflower's Mercies* teach methods by which those who serve Sarenrae as soldiers can vanquish enemies in combat without killing them, and encourage those who follow the teachings held within to offer those they take prisoner the chance to be welcomed into Sarenrae's arms.

Initial Benefit: You take no penalty on attack rolls for using a scimitar to deal nonlethal damage. If your attack with the scimitar would normally deal additional damage (such as via sneak attack, the *flaming* weapon special ability, or the like), this additional damage can be nonlethal damage. You can also alter spells with the fire, good, or light descriptor and inflict spells so that the damage they deal is nonlethal damage instead. You can choose to apply this effect as the spell is cast.

Advanced Prerequisites: Great Fortitude, Weapon Focus (scimitar), Heal 10 ranks.

Advanced Benefit: Once per round as you strike a foe with a weapon and deal nonlethal damage with that attack, you regain 1d6 hit points as the warmth of Sarenrae's approval and the conviction that you are doing the right thing to minimize suffering infuses your body and soul. If the attack that dealt nonlethal damage was from a scimitar, you instead regain 2d6 hit points. You can gain the benefit of this healing only once per round, regardless of how many successful attacks you make with the weapon.

TORAG'S PATIENT STRIKES

Copies of *Lessons of the Father*, the divine fighting manual of Torag, are somewhat rare outside of the Five Kings Mountains, as tradition mandates that all copies of *Lessons of the Father* must be scribed by hand in Dwarven on iron sheets and bound between slabs of stone hand-carved by a cleric of Torag. As a result, these tomes are somewhat cumbersome to transport (even the smallest copy of the book weighs 50 pounds, and most exceed 100 pounds in weight). Those who have mastered the *Lessons of the Father* are highly respected within the faith.

Initial Benefit: Whenever you wield a warhammer, add your Wisdom bonus to the total number of attacks of opportunity that you can make per round. These additional attacks of opportunity don't stack with those granted by Combat Reflexes, but this benefit counts as Combat Reflexes for the purpose of satisfying feat prerequisites and prestige class requirements. In addition, you can make attacks of opportunity while you're flat-footed.

Advanced Prerequisites: Divine Fighting Technique, Vital Strike, Weapon Focus (warhammer), base attack bonus +10.

Advanced Benefit: Once per round, before you make an attack of opportunity with a warhammer, you can declare an opportunistic strike. If the attack hits, you can apply the effects of your Vital Strike feat. You can apply the Improved Vital Strike or Greater Vital Strike feat instead if you have either of those feats. If you confirm a critical hit with an opportunistic strike, you can attempt a disarm or trip combat maneuver check against the target as a free action—this combat maneuver does not provoke an attack of opportunity.

URGATHOA'S HUNGER

The grisly content of *Pallid Cravings* can be found in many places where the Pallid Princess maintains a significant presence, especially within the undead nation of Geb. The pages of this manuscript are said to be tattooed onto a humanoid and flensed off while the victim is still alive; the swaths of skin are then carefully preserved for presentation in the book. *Pallid Cravings* details hundreds of ways for a member of Urgathoa's faithful to satisfy her depraved urges for an opponent's flesh and blood while in battle.

Initial Benefit: A number of times per day equal to your Wisdom bonus, you can feast upon the life essence of a creature that you hit with a scythe. Activating this ability is a swift action. When you do so, you gain a number of temporary hit points equal to the damage you dealt with the scythe attack. These temporary hit points last for 1 minute and don't stack.

Advanced Prerequisites: Divine Fighting Technique, Heal 10 ranks, base attack bonus +7.

Advanced Benefit: A number of times per day equal to your Wisdom bonus, you can exacerbate any lingering contagions within a target's body upon making a successful melee attack with a scythe. Activating this ability is a swift action, and causes the target to immediately attempt additional saving throws against all diseases with which it is currently afflicted. Any failed saves cause the target to immediately take the effects of that disease, while a successful save does not count toward the number of consecutive saves that the target must succeed at in order to cure the disease.

Next Month!

There are far more fantasy races than elves and dwarves! *Pathfinder Player Companion: Blood of the Beast* explores seven such races: catfolk, gripplis, kitsune, nagaji, ratfolk, tengus, and vanaras. Each receives an examination of its place in Golarion and expanded options that characters of many races can use, such as the luck magic of catfolk and the ki powers that vanaras have perfected.

Would You Like to Know More?

The power offered by the sacred tomes presented in these pages is a small fraction what can be found in prayer or in the pages of ancient books. The following Pathfinder products further explore many sources of such wondrous abilities!

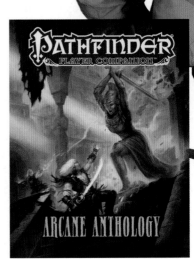

Learn about dozens of Golarion's awe-inspiring deities and demigods and unlock the myriad powers of your character's faith with *Pathfinder Campaign Setting: Inner Sea Gods*!

The faithful of the Inner Sea region also worship many local deities. Check out *Pathfinder Campaign Setting: Inner Sea Faiths* to learn about these deities and their holy books and dogmas.

While *Divine Anthology* focuses on servants of divine powers, *Pathfinder Player Companion: Arcane Anthology* is packed with spellbooks and eldritch lore for those pursuing arcane might.